Computer Networks

Philip J Irving

Lexden Publishing Ltd

Dedication

This book is dedicated to the special people in my life who made this all possible: Elizabeth, Victoria Rose, Philip, Margaret, Frank, Ena, Pat and Keith. Thanks for your help and support. Special thanks to Dave Nelson and Dave Ho for their keen eye and willingness to help.

Second Edition published in 2005 by Lexden Publishing Ltd.

First Edition published in 2003 by Crucial, a division of Learning Matters Ltd.

© Philip J Irving

British Library Cataloguing in Publication Data

A CIP record for this book is available from the British Library.

ISBN-10: 1 904995 08 X

ISBN-13: 978 1 904995 08 1

Printed in Great Britain by Athenaeum Press Ltd.

Lexden Publishing Ltd, 23 Irvine Road, Colchester, Essex C03 3TS

Tel: 01206 533164

Email: info@lexden-publishing.co.uk

www.lexden-publishing.co.uk

Contents

Also from Lexden Publishing:

Title	Author	ISBN
Computer Systems Architecture	R Newman, E Gaura, D Hibbs	1-903337-07-0
Databases	R Warrender	1-903337-08-9
JavaScript: Creating Dynamic Web Pages	E Gandy, S Stobart	1-904995-07-1
Multimedia Computing	D Cunliffe, G Elliott	1-904995-05-5
User Interface Design	J Le Peuple, R Scane	1-903337-19-4
Visual Programming	D Leigh	1-903337-11-9

These books are written for students studying degree programmes, HND courses and foundation degrees in Computing and Information Technology.

To order, please call our order hotline on 01202 712909 or visit our website at www.lexden-publishing.co.uk for further information.

Introduction

Computer Networks

Networking is a strange subject to study – it moves at such a rapid pace that it seems that just as you become familiar with the technology, it becomes outdated and is replaced. If we liken the development of Ethernet performance over the last 10 years to cars, a car that could do 100 mph in 1992 would, in 2005, be doing 100,000 mph. As is usual for computing, the price would also fall dramatically. Working solely on cost, if a car cost £20,000 in 1994, the better equivalent would retail in 2005 for £40.

In case you didn't realise, Networking is the fastest growing area of computing and despite efforts there is still a large skills shortage. At the time of writing, preliminary results of a Cisco commissioned IDC survey showed that there was a shortfall of over 55,000 full-time networking staff across Europe with an estimate of 173,000 skilled individuals needed, which is expected to rise to 288,000 by 2008. The survey shows an even greater skills shortage of specialised network professionals (VoIP, CCNP, wireless, etc.). Average salaries in networking are also high – the average salary for a Cisco Certified Networking Associate (CCNA) being £30,000 and for a Cisco Certified Networking Professional (CCNP) being £70,000.

Which courses does the book cover?

This book has been designed for students studying general networking and will be useful to any course that covers computer networking. Networking is a huge subject and as a student studying general networking, depth of coverage is neither what you need nor want. Instead, this book provides a solid overview of general networking, explaining the concepts and providing you with enough information to study successfully at least five possible courses:

● EDEXCEL Computer Networking module;

● General Degree networking module;

● General Foundation Degree networking module;

● General Masters degree networking module;

● Basic introduction to Computer Networking perhaps as preparation for, or accompanying, CCNA courses.

This book is intended to provide you with enough theory to aid your understanding and, where possible, with some practical skills – for example, *Chapter 7* gives you the basic practical skills to analyse and design small computer networks.

Learning outcomes

Almost all UK courses of study in networking are aligned with the Quality Assurance Agency (QAA) code of practice, which requires learning outcomes to be specified for each module of a programme and the programme overall. This book is aligned with this practice and, at the beginning of each chapter you will find details of the learning outcomes addressed. Overall, the book covers the following learning outcomes:

● To understand network principles, applications and VoIP definitions of a computer network, including remote access, email, cost/benefits, intranets, extranets and the Internet.

● To understand networking resources, including facilities provided, hardware, software, security, constraints, performance and licensing.

- To understand and be able to undertake the design and evaluation of computer networks, including the ISO 7 layer model, topologies, communication devices, popular technologies (including wireless), the TCP/IP model, capacity planning and network design.

- To be able to undertake simple management of computer networks – management of users, groups, workgroups, security implications and responsibilities. Elements of good practice concerning computer viruses, monitoring, estimating resource usage and connection to the outside world.

- To understand the basic principles involved in setting up a computer network including the basic steps of installation and customisation of Linux and developing login scripts, file systems and file system security.

- To understand the need for network and system security and be able to evaluate network security; devise, implement and monitor security policies.

Using learning outcomes to plan your study

Learning outcomes are intended to be assessed directly, and you must demonstrate competence in them all. Be careful here – if you pass one out of two assignments with 100% and decide to skip the second, you will most probably fail as you haven't demonstrated competence in all learning outcomes. **The bottom line is: don't miss an assessment**.

There are two possible ways you can be assessed: either by an assignment/practical or by a time-constrained test (TCT) or exam. Your assignment comes first, and you can use the content of the assignment to cross off the learning outcomes it covers – in some institutions the learning outcomes covered are printed on the front of the assignment. As there is little point in assessing the same learning outcome twice, you will therefore have a fairly good idea what is going to be covered in the exam/TCT.

Networking has both practical and theoretical elements to it. Most institutions do not have the resources to allow students to set up a computer network or to 'play' with the equipment. As such, practical assessments are likely to be limited to designing a computer network, to producing a user guide on the installation of a networked operating system or to undertaking a capacity planning exercise. The theoretical aspects lend themselves to being covered in the exam/TCT.

What's in the book

In a nutshell, this book covers the basics you would need to know if studying a general computer networking module as part of any further or higher education course of study. If you are studying a specialist course (for example networked computing), you will still find it a useful study guide but will certainly require more depth in certain areas, which should be apparent from the lectures you attend.

Tips and tricks

The main tips and tricks associated with studying computer networking are as follows:

- Get used to memorising and drawing diagrams – they help you understand, explain and demonstrate your understanding to the examiner.

- Try to learn a phrase or saying that will help you remember sequences or theories (this book offers a number of suggestions).

- Try to think of an everyday example of the item you are studying (this book offers a number of suggestions).

- Ensure you understand the key parts before you move on.

- Maintain a log book of acronyms and their meaning. Try to commit these to memory (*see Glossary*).

- Ask when you are unsure.

Textbooks

Rather than specify textbooks for further study at the beginning of the book, I have recommended further reading on a chapter-by-chapter basis. A general tip would be to avoid the large computer networking books if you are only studying the subjects at an introductory level – they are likely to confuse rather than help you.

Additional materials and resources

An additional chapter, *Revision*, is available to download from the publisher's website. This chapter offers advice on tackling assignment questions, marking schemes and sample multiple choice questions.

To obtain this chapter and view other resources please visit:
www.lexden-publishing.co.uk/it/computernetworks

Additional material is also available from the author's website:
www.philipirving.com

Good luck in your studies.

Key to symbols used in this book

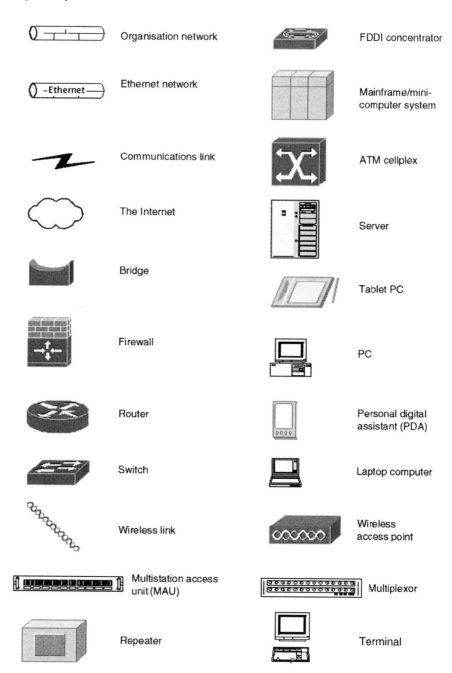

Organisation network	FDDI concentrator
Ethernet network	Mainframe/mini-computer system
Communications link	ATM cellplex
The Internet	Server
Bridge	Tablet PC
Firewall	PC
Router	Personal digital assistant (PDA)
Switch	Laptop computer
Wireless link	Wireless access point
Multistation access unit (MAU)	Multiplexor
Repeater	Terminal

Symbols courtesy of Cisco Networking Academy

Chapter 1
Introduction to networks

Chapter summary

This chapter provides an introduction to computer networks and networking. When studying computer networking, it is important to understand that it has evolved and will continue to evolve. As new technologies become available, the uses to which that technology is being put (and can be put) will also evolve. A computer network can be categorised according to the geographical area it covers as well as by the type of access it provides to the outside world.

Learning outcomes

After studying this chapter you should aim to test your achievement of the following outcomes. You should be able to:

Outcome 1: Evolution of networks

Understand the way in which computer networks have evolved and the principal stages of this evolution. Question 1 at the end of this chapter will test your ability to do this.

Outcome 2: Two main types of networked computing

Understand the two main categories of computer networking and be able to describe the differences. Question 2 at the end of this chapter will test your ability to do this.

Outcome 3: Network categories

Understand and be able to describe what is meant by the terms LAN, WAN, MAN, PAN, VAN, VLAN, VPN, VoIP, intranet, Internet and extranet. Question 3 at the end of this chapter will test your ability to do this.

How will you be assessed on this?

Assessors want you to demonstrate your knowledge; they don't want you to regurgitate the contents of a book. By understanding networks and their evolution you will be better placed to demonstrate your knowledge. The subject matter of this chapter could be assessed on its own (see the end of chapter questions) or it could be linked with the answer to another question.

TIPS & ADVICE

Diagrams, diagrams, and diagrams! Computer networking is complex and becomes even more complex the more we study it. One of the key ways of picking up marks and saving time in assessments is to use diagrams. A diagram in networking is 'worth a thousand words'. Diagrams aren't particularly difficult to memorise and will impress the assessor with your command of the subject.

Section 1: The evolution of computer networks

Computer networks have been evolving for almost half a century. During this time organisations have become critically dependent upon the services provided by these networks and, today, there are few organisations that could survive without them. This section traces the milestones in the evolution of computer networks.

What are computer networks?

There are many definitions of computer networks but they all have one thing in common: a computer network facilitates the exchange (and processing) of data (and information) between two or more interconnected devices (or points/nodes).

Early computer systems

The earliest computer systems usually comprised a mainframe computer that had little or no interaction with other machines (*Figure 1.1*). The costs of this equipment were huge and so the time spent working on them had to be maximised to justify the costs involved. However, the processing power of these machines was extremely limited (probably not more than equivalent of today's average digital watch). Programmers produced punched cards or paper tape containing code, whilst data-input clerks produced punch tapes (or paper tape) of the data to be input into the machine. These tapes were then taken to the 'machine room' where the computer was housed, were fed in, processed and the results printed out.

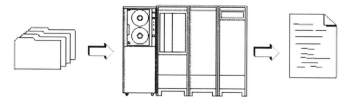

**Figure 1.1: Early computer systems
(diagram courtesy of Prof. J. Tait, University of Sunderland)**

These early computer systems had enormous benefits for the large organisations that owned them. Routine systems, such as payroll, sales and purchase order processing, were amongst the first systems to be computerised. However, the benefits they brought – although huge – were limited by the manner in which the programs and data had to be fed into the computer, and there was no interactive computing – everything was fed in via punched cards (or paper tape).

The code these earlier programmers used was in a format people could not read. It was put on to punched cards or paper tape and fed into the machine for compilation or execution. Compilation and logic errors were then printed, and the programmers had to work 'offline' on these error messages, amending the punched cards and often rekeying the batch. Today, editing and recompiling code are done online, as a result of the development of networks. Hence a modern programmer's time is used more efficiently than that of early programmers. It was not long, therefore, before the demand grew for more interaction with the computer.

> **KEY CONCEPT**
>
> In early systems, all the equipment was in one room and was controlled totally by the computer operators. There was no connectivity outside the computer room.

Local interactive terminals

As computer systems developed, their processing power increased and they were given secondary storage (tapes, disks). In terms of networks this phase of development was important. Although early computers had a main console, terminals were now attached to computer systems for the first time. Often in the form of a teletype (a combined printer and typewriter), these terminals enabled users to interact with the computer. The terminals were connected directly to the computer and were in the same area of the building as the mainframe computer (*Figure 1.2*). These links were nearly always made using serial lines (RS232), which meant a limited distance (typically a maximum of 15 m or 45 ft) and limited speed but none the less, they heralded the first computer network. Interactive computing was born and programmers could now edit, compile and execute their code online.

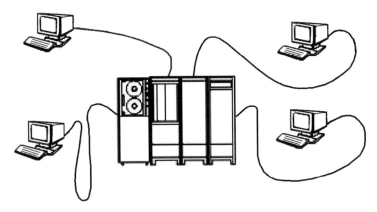

Figure 1.2: Local interactive terminals
(diagram courtesy of Prof. J. Tait, University of Sunderland)

A further important advance occurred in the operating system. Previously, operating systems would typically only support one user and one task (single user, single tasking). Now the operating system had to support multiple users and multiple tasks (multi-user, multitasking). (A full discussion of the types of operating systems can be found in *Chapter 8*.)

> **KEY CONCEPT**
> Local users could now edit and control the running of their own programs.

Remote access

As the concept of interactive computing became more widely known, people in other buildings and at other sites also wanted to gain access to the computers. A method was developed to support this – terminals were connected via modems (modulator/demodu-lators) and telephone lines (*Figure 1.3*). These allowed the use of normal dial-up telephone lines as simple (unfortunately, though, slow and unreliable), long-distance computer connections.

Just as they are today, modems were used to connect the terminals and remote computer systems to a telephone line, carrying the data over a line designed to carry voice traffic. Hence, the modem carried out a digital-to-analogue conversion. The speed of these modems was about 300 bits per second (bps), compared with today's typical speeds of 56,000 bps. However, the volume of data transmitted was not great, as these devices worked only in characters.

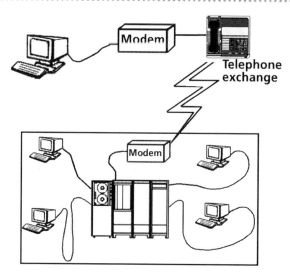

**Figure 1.3: Remote modem connections
(diagram courtesy of Prof. J. Tait, University of Sunderland)**

The telephone lines were provided by telecomms providers (such as BT) and were normal telephone lines in almost every sense – they passed through normal telephone exchanges and could be dialled up. Programmers and users no longer needed to work in the same building as the computer, and so many large organisations used this technology to provide terminals in their local offices. For example, electricity companies provided terminals at their local branches and local authorities installed terminals in their libraries for automated library systems.

KEY CONCEPT

Users were now able to access the computer system remotely through a telephone line. Organisations were able to use this technology to provide remote access to branch offices.

Leased lines

By the middle to late 1970s many larger organisations had more than one computer and their staff needed regular access to data and computing facilities at sites other than their base. The scale of communication, as well as the required speed and reliability, meant that modem connection through the ordinary, switched telephone network could no longer support their needs. This led to the adoption of permanently connected long-distance lines between two end points terminating in an organisation's own premises (usually provided by telephone companies). Such lines could span the country or even the world. These connections are known as leased lines (*Figure 1.4*) and are still offered by most communication service providers today although, in practice, they rarely offer the fixed wire copper connection of years gone by. Leased line networks were the first real wide area networks and were the forerunners of packet switched networks and Asynchronous Transfer Mode (ATM) networks.

Leased lines were analogue and, as such, still required modems. However, the modems used were high quality and high speed, delivering up to 14,400 bps. The links were secure and costs were based on line rental rather than call costs. Usually, their capacity was far in excess of the capacity needed by a single terminal and, to utilise the line to its fullest, multiplexors were developed and added to either end of the link. The purpose of a multiplexor is to share the line capacity amongst a number of terminals. In *Figure*

1.5 there are two terminals connected to a multiplexor. As the multiplexor is a simple Time Division Multiplexor (TDM) it will share the time slot (e.g. 1 second) between the two terminals in short bursts. Therefore each terminal will get half the time slot, in this instance, half a second each. The multiplexors at each end of the line are synchronised with each other, ensuring that the correct data is passed down the correct time slot. In practice, eight terminals would be typically linked through a multiplexor. This arrangement was common up until the mid-1990s.

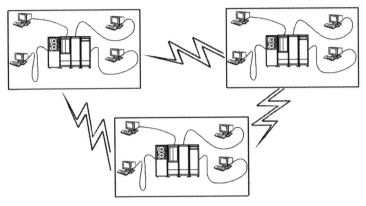

Figure 1.4: Leased line networks
(diagram courtesy of Prof. J. Tait, University of Sunderland)

Leased lines continued to extend the benefits networks were offering organisations. Heralding the first, real, Wide Area Network (WAN), they allowed more access from remote locations (such as local offices) through the sharing of a private line. Utility companies and local authorities deployed such systems to give local offices access to the centrally held information. It is important to note, however, that such access cannot be considered client/server (*see Section 2*) as the users are using dumb terminals (terminals with no computing power) – simply a monitor and a keyboard.

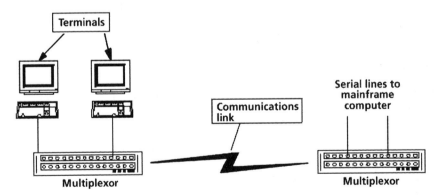

Figure 1.5: Leased line arrangement using multiplexors

KEY CONCEPT

Leased lines provided remote users with high-security, high-speed dedicated links, which increased the opportunities for remote access to the computer system.

Local area networks

By the late 1970s many organisations (large and small) had more than one computer. This trend accelerated rapidly in the early 1980s with the availability of powerful (for that time) stand-alone personal computers (PCs) – a trend that continues to the present day. The method of access at this time meant that users needed one terminal per system, but demand grew for PCs to be able to access many systems (including other PCs) and to transfer files. This led to the need for a system that was capable of transferring data at high speed between different sorts of computers typically located close together at the same site or in the same building.

This need was answered by the development of modern high-speed Local Area Networks (LANs), such as Ethernet and Token Ring. The mid-1980s saw the introduction of these in many organisations, but they came into even more widespread use in the 1990s. These technologies bridge the gap between high-speed computer-room networks (parallel interfaces, etc.) and low-speed serial interfaces (e.g. RS-232) (*see the earlier section 'Local interactive terminals'*). They allowed multiple devices to be connected via a shared transmission medium (*Figure 1.6*). Since their inception, a number of LAN technologies have been developed and, in the early days, there were a number of standards for LANs, including Arcnet (for the BBC micros) and the Cambridge ring. As often happens, the market has largely settled on a few technologies, primarily Ethernet but also Token Ring (these will be discussed in detail in *Chapters 3* and *5*). LANs further extended the benefits networks offer by allowing the interconnection of multiple computing facilities (such as PCs, mainframes and mini-computers) through a high-speed link.

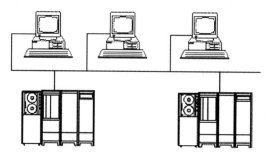

Figure 1.6: Local area networks
(diagram courtesy of Prof. J. Tait, University of Sunderland)

KEY CONCEPT

LANs provided easy-to-establish, high-speed connectivity between any connected devices, but with limited distances.

Quick test
Briefly outline the major stages in the evolution of networks.

Section 2: Types of networked computing

The main purpose of computer networking is to provide an organisation with services. Initially, this was for interactive computing but, with the introduction of PCs, the network has evolved to allow communication between PCs and also to provide services such as shared printing, shared disk access, etc. Networks typically provide these services to a client from either a dedicated server (known as client/server computing or networking) or from a peer computer (known as peer-to-peer networking). Networks constructed with a server are often said to have a client/server architecture, and those with a community of equals are often said to have a peer-to-peer architecture. Understanding these architectures is fundamental to the study of networking.

Introduction

All networked computing facilities can be grouped into two architectures:

- peer-to-peer networking;
- client/server networking.

Both architectures are intended for different uses and require networked operating systems (NOS) support (now built into Microsoft Windows).

> **KEY CONCEPT**
>
> The fundamental difference between the two architectures is that client/server architectures require a dedicated server whereas, with peer-to-peer networks, there is no separate server and the work of the server is shared between the connected computers. Comparing *Figures 1.7* and *1.8* (*see below*) you will notice that *Figure 1.8* does not have a server. However, the physical connections to the media are still the same.

Client/server computing

This is the traditional model of networked computing (*Figure 1.7*). Here clients make requests of a server (the diagrams shows a single-server system) and the server then carries out the request and provides a response to the client. This model has been in operation for many years and we have all probably encountered it at some point. It is 'full blown' networking architecture and is supported by all network operating system vendors, such as Novell and even Microsoft in Windows NT and 2000. It is also supported by all versions of UNIX.

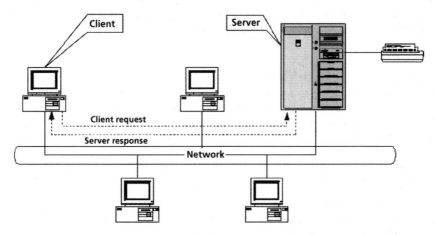

Figure 1.7: Typical client/server architecture

Key to this architecture is that there is (at least) one serving computer (the server) which provides all the client machines with the facilities they need – usually file and printer sharing. Although these services might seem trivial, they revolutionised computing. Without a network, sharing files was a real problem requiring users to share a floppy disk. As can be imagined, many problems arise from sharing a floppy disk, the most obvious being, of course, the inconvenience of having physically to take the disk to the other user. Others include the compatibility and reliability of floppy disks and their limited capacity. In some cases, sharing a floppy disk is impossible – consider a gig or cinema booking system with multiple users trying to access the same file: could they really operate by sharing a floppy disk?

Specialist printers (such as colour laser printers) can be expensive and might not be used very often. By attaching such devices to a server, their facilities are made available to all network users, giving everyone access with minimal inconvenience.

As the client/server architecture and its supporting Network Operating Systems (commonly called a NOS) have developed, other facilities have been added. For example, users can now be allocated to groups and security can be increased through the allocation of rights to those groups, granting access to specific files or devices. Files can also be accessed simultaneously by many users (although locking controls need to be in place to stop two users updating the same record at the same time). Printers have queues , which allow a client machine to send its entire print job to the server for processing – thus freeing up the client machine's own processing capacity. Some NOSs work on different types of computers allowing the machines to 'talk' to each other. An example of this is Novell Netware, which is available for Mac and PC platforms. Email facilities also require a central server.

Client/server computing has undoubtedly revolutionised computing and provides benefits almost all organisations desire. The advantages far outweigh the disadvantages. The principal disadvantage, however, is cost – with client/server computing, there is a need to purchase a central serving machine that should be fast and have huge storage capacity. Such machines are not cheap and this sometimes puts them out of the reach of smaller businesses – enter the alternative approach of peer-to-peer networking!

One other disadvantage to client/server computing is the reliance upon one central system for the provision of services. If something happens to that machine, access to all the information and to the services of that machine is lost. Therefore, competent personnel are required to manage client/server architectures.

KEY CONCEPT

With client server network architectures, there is (at least one) server that is a dedicated machine providing services to the client. This machine may be unusable other than through one of its client computers.

Peer-to-peer networking

Peer-to-peer networking is a low-cost way of providing some of the more popular benefits of networks at a fraction of the cost of a full-blown NOS. Its major benefit is, again, the sharing of resources printers, files, faxes, etc. The fundamental difference between client/server and peer-to-peer computing, however, is that with peer-to-peer networks, there is no central server (*Figure 1.8*). The tasks a server would normally perform are shared between the client machines themselves. For example, a shared printer would be connected to a client machine rather than being connected to the server. Similarly, data to be shared would reside on a client machine rather than on the server. Often all that is needed to establish a peer-to-peer network is the network cabling itself and a version of an operating system that supports peer-to-peer networking (e.g. Windows 3.11, 95, 98, 2000, XP, etc.).

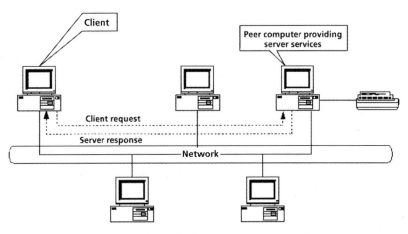

Figure 1.8: Typical peer-to-peer network

Peer-to-peer networks obtain their name from the fact that, while each machine is being used by a user (a client), it may also be serving another computer (therefore acting as a server). Thus the conventional terms 'client' or 'server' are not applicable as, in this network, the machines are a community of 'equals' (peers). As there is no requirement for an expensive server and the machines usually have the appropriate software installed, peer-to-peer networking is a low-cost solution for smaller businesses or isolated pockets in large organisations. Because this type of networking is often found in small offices, it is sometimes referred to as 'small office computing'.

Whilst it is possible to have a peer-to-peer network of large servers (e.g. UNIX servers), this is not generally what is meant by the definition of peer-to-peer networking and certainly not what is meant here. Peer-to-peer networking is really only suitable for small installations. Microsoft recommends a maximum of ten computers. After this, not only will throughput deteriorate, but also the general performance of the machines. It is not possible to give an exact figure because it depends upon how the computers are being used – if lots of disk and file sharing is going on, performance issues may arise with only four computers. Conversely, if there is little sharing of devices, both the network and the computers might operate satisfactorily with up to ten or more machines.

TIPS & ADVICE

Microsoft recommends a maximum of ten machines in a peer-to-peer network.

The vendors of peer-to-peer network operating systems have made their set-up very simple, thus avoiding the need for specialist network management skills. Overall, peer-to-peer networks are most useful to smaller organisations that wish to try out networking in a small way or to larger organisations wishing to solve small problems. Usually there is little or no planning; such environments are usually fairly stable in terms of the user base; and peer to peer networks are only used for sharing a few resources. Examples would be a Managing Director and a Personal Assistant (PA) in a large organisation who link their machines to transfer data (files, letters, reports, etc.) and small office computing (e.g. a small law firm or a small estate agent who require file and printer sharing). Whilst isolated pockets in large organisations are not recommended, peer-to-peer networking can sometimes help provide limited connectivity as a stop-gap measure until the IT department is able to connect all the users. Small businesses, on the other hand, can use peer-to-peer networking whilst they expand and grow. The relatively low start-up costs, however, must be weighed against the possibilities for limited expansion, although investment in a company's peer-to-peer technology would not necessarily be lost when it was big enough to expand into a full client/server situation.

Peer-to-peer networking has many advantages for the small organisation, but it also has its disadvantages. In a client/server network, the server is a powerful machine, reflecting the amount of work it does. If a peer-to-peer network is installed instead, the processing normally associated with a server has to be undertaken by the client machines themselves. This means that, as well as processing the task in hand, the machine must also undertake additional processing at someone else's request. Ultimately, this results in an overall degeneration in the machine's performance.

Security is also an issue. Whilst peer-to-peer NOS manufacturers have made setting up these networks relatively easy, they have placed security in the hands of inexperienced users who might be unaware of the consequences of their actions. Therefore, there are often glaring security gaps in such installations.

The random distribution of resources can be a further problem with peer-to-peer networking. If the data is shared among many machines and one fails or cannot be started, it can be difficult to predict the consequences of such failure. For example, peer-to-peer networking often won't begin until a certain user has logged into his or her computer. Imagine a situation in a small business where someone powers off his or her PC on a Friday evening before going on holiday for two weeks. If that machine cannot be started without the password, no one in the organisation can access the data on it. If the data is payroll information, no one might be paid until the user returns from holiday. For security reasons, however, the password should not be shared.

> **KEY CONCEPT**
>
> With peer-to-peer networking, it is the method of accessing resources that differs from client/server networking. In peer-to-peer networking, there's no server, and access to files, printers and other resources is provided by the user machines.

Summary

Both client/server and peer-to-peer networking have their advantages and disadvantages and careful consideration should be given to these when choosing the correct one for an organisation. It is always best to choose a client/server architecture unless there are compelling reasons for choosing a peer-to-peer network. It is also important to note that both architectures need a network technology (cables, cards, etc.) to operate on (technologies are covered in *Chapter 3*).

Quick test

Briefly list the differences between client/server and peer-to-peer network architectures.

Section 3: Network categories

Networks can be classified into four distinct types, although the boundaries between these types are somewhat blurred. This section reviews the different categories of network and identifies the key differences between them.

Introduction

Networks are often classified into four types depending upon the geographical area they cover and according to some other distinguishing factors. It is necessary to understand the differences between them in terms of performance, geographic coverage, limitations of connection speed and degree of choice in the service provided, etc. The four common categories are:

- Local Area Networks (LANs);
- Metropolitan Area Networks (MANs);
- Wide Area Networks (WANs);
- Personal Area Networks (PANs)

– although a new category is emerging – Vehicular Area Networks (VANs). There are also other terms – Virtual Local Area Networks (VLANs) and Virtual Private Networks (VPNs).

Local area network (LAN)

Local area networks (or LANs, as they are called) cover, with the exception of PANs, the smallest geographical area for networks. Despite this, they are the most popular category, and LANs often have hundreds if not thousands of connections. LANs, as their name suggests, are intended to be local and small, although now this is not necessarily the case. When this type of network was first devised, a typical LAN would have been a classroom, an office or, at most, a few offices. Now LANs cover entire floors or even entire buildings and with buildings such as universities, colleges and call centres that is a lot of connections!

LANs usually offer the highest speed of all network types as the media used in such networks are controlled by the organisations themselves and so, any constraints on the implementation of the technology are the responsibility of the organisations. For example, an organisation in the middle of the countryside is free to implement whatever media it desires for its LAN: it simply needs to buy the necessary equipment and install it. It could also have whatever speed LAN current technology supports. Should it wish to connect to a telecommunications provider (e.g. BT), the speed of connection would then be limited to what the provider can offer, which, in some parts of the countryside, is likely to be limited.

> **KEY CONCEPT**
>
> The characteristics of a LAN are as follows:
> - It is usually based in one building.
> - The speed of the technology is at the organisation's discretion.
> - The management and maintenance of the network are the organisation's responsibility.
> - There is a choice of technology.
> - There is no outside involvement from telecommunications providers.

Metropolitan area networks (MANs)

MANs are larger than LANs, yet they are contained within a defined geographical area. A good example of a MAN is a university campus where several buildings are connected together across a city or town or several universities or colleges are connected across a region. The media used in a MAN may be the jurisdiction of the organisation itself or may belong to one or more telecomms providers (in which case the speed may be restricted). The real determining factor in who provides the media, however, is cost. Although UK law currently allows for any organisation to lay its own cables, the cost of doing so safely and without risk to the public is high. The longer the cable run, the more expensive this becomes, and so it is often cheaper to contract with a telecomms provider who can provide the link at a lower cost.

MANs frequently don't belong to a single organisation but are a city or regional resource. An example of this is the NORthern Metropolitan Area Network (NORman), which is a network in the North East of England linking together the universities in the area and providing them with a very high-speed Internet connection. Because they use the services of a telecomms provider, MANs usually run at a slower speed than a LAN. However, they span a larger geographic area than a LAN and are either managed/maintained by both the organisation and the telecomms provider or are the sole responsibility of the organisation.

MANs cover the ground somewhere between LANs and WANs (*see the next section*). They can be contained within an organisation's site or they may be a regional resource. They generally operate on lines leased from a communications provider and, hence, operate at a lower speed than a LAN.

Wide area networks (WANs)

WANs cover a geographical area beyond that of a MAN – perhaps all an organisation's offices in a country or even beyond national boundaries (a good example would be a multinational organisation with offices in different countries). WANs are almost always dependent upon telecomms providers, as the length of the media runs are huge and prohibitively expensive.

As WANs are dependent upon telecomms providers, the speed of the link is likely to be limited compared with a MAN or a LAN. For example, the fastest commonly available link (in 2005) on a LAN is 1 Gbps or 1000 Mbps, and the cost of the equipment to set up a two-station network would be around £70 (at 2005 prices). In contrast, the current fastest link on a WAN is also 1 Gbps, but costs about £42,000 per annum to lease (at 2005 prices) for the first 10 km, then £2000/km. For connection, the costs are £52,500 for the first 10 km and then £1000/km.

Until 1998 the fastest link available externally was only about 2 Mbps, and this speed (or slower) can still be encountered in many parts of the world where a WAN may have to make a link. Maintenance of the WAN is shared between the organisation and the telecomms provider. When selecting a WAN link it is important to ensure that the provider will correct any faults in a timely manner – especially if the organisation is critically dependent upon the link.

TIPS & ADVICE

Just as a chain is only as strong as its weakest link, so the speed of a network is usually only as fast as its slowest link – thoroughly research the areas where you wish to deploy a WAN.

KEY CONCEPT

WANS are differentiated in the following ways:
- By the large geographic area they cover.
- They almost always use a telecomms provider.
- They are slower than a MAN or LAN link.
- They possibly depend upon a number of telecomms providers (if they are international networks).
- Maintenance is shared between the telecomms provider and the organisation.

Personal area networks (PANs)

The PAN definition started around the year 2000. PANs are intended to link personal computing devices such as Personal Digital Assistants (PDAs), mobile phones and laptops within a personal area – absolute maximum of 10 metres. PANs are intended to do away with the wires we all carry to link devices via a wireless network. Each of the devices is fitted with a radio communications card (working in Ghz), which allows it to communicate with several other devices simultaneously. One of the better known PAN technologies is Bluetooth. Bluetooth is a consortium of manufacturers that developed a standard that allows connection worldwide. More information can be found at **www.bluetooth.com**.

Bluetooth has enjoyed a rapid take-up and is used in a wide range of devices including mobile phones (handsets and headsets), digital video cameras and digital cameras as well as PDAs and laptops. Indeed, some car manufacturers have built in Bluetooth mobile phone connections. One of the likely limiting factors to Bluetooth is its speed. In 2005, Bluetooth operated at a maximum 1 Mbps.

In 2005, the USB alliance (**www.usb.org**) launched a wireless USB standard 'for next generation consumer electronic devices'. Speeds quoted are 480 Mbps at 3 m and 110 Mbps at 10 metres. Given the vastly superior speeds offered, wireless USB is likely to become the future PAN technology.

TIPS & ADVICE

One of the most common mistakes made by students is to forget that networks are measured in megabits per second (Mbps) and that data is measured in megabytes (MB). There are 8 bits in a byte and failure to work in bits rather than bytes puts you out by a factor of 8. Thus 1 MB of data to be transferred is 8 Mb.

Vehicular area networks (VANs)

The VAN definition started around the year 2004. VANs are usually wireless networks whose reach is bounded by the vehicle in which they are deployed. For example, in the UK, Virgin and GNER trains have wireless LANs that are available to train passengers throughout their journey.

As the travelling public demand Internet access, VANs are sure to become commonplace on aircraft as well as buses and other forms of public transport.

Technically, VANs are just wireless networks (*see Chapter 5*) that are available within a vehicle. The access point is located somewhere within the vehicle maintaining the connection for those travelling inside the vehicle. The actual connection to the Internet is made separately from the vehicle using a variety of technologies.

Virtual local area networks (VLANs)

Often, an organisation wishes to subdivide its LAN – for example, the accounts or personnel department may wish to keep its network secure whilst still being connected to the organisational LAN. This can be achieved using VLANs. VLAN technology is a by-product of switching technology (*see Chapter 6*), allowing a LAN to be subdivided into several virtual LANs. There is no difference in the physical structure of the LAN, but the switches deployed are configured to segregate traffic. *Figure 1.9* shows a typical VLAN configuration. Here the network is divided into three separate VLANs. As with a normal LAN, the data passes through the organisation's backbone but, this time, it is tagged, identifying the VLAN to which it belongs. Data is only distributed within the VLAN, which provides greater security.

VLANs can be configured in one of two ways:

- Making the switch port a member of the VLAN. Thus any computer plugged into the port will become a member of that VLAN. This is known as a port centric.

- Via the MAC address (*see Chapter 3*). Each machine has a unique address (called the MAC address). This can be used to determine VLAN membership. Thus VLAN membership is determined by the computer's MAC address, irrespective of the port to which it is connected. This is more secure than port centric as a potential hacker would need to gain access to a computer that is a member of the VLAN. This type of configuration is known as dynamic.

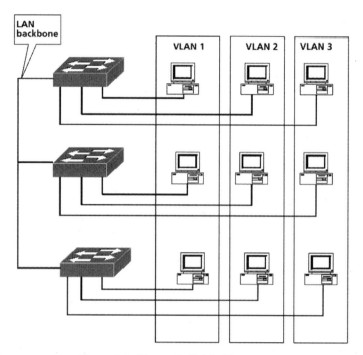

Figure 1.9: Network divided into VLANs

Intranets/Internet

Networks are also classified according to their connection to the 'general public'. Categorised as intranets, the Internet and extranets, this classification can be used to determine whether access to the network is from a closed group or from all groups.

Intranet

Intranets are networks that provide the facilities we have come to expect from the World Wide Web, such as web pages, file transfer, form filling, etc., but they provide these to a closed group only, normally controlled by a password. For example, the XYZ Widget company may have several sales executives travelling and meeting with customers. As support for these executives, the company wants them to have access to production schedules, customer information and costing details. If they had been based in the company offices, the network would provide them with this information. As the information will constantly change, it isn't feasible continuously to send them disks containing the information. Using the Internet would solve the problem but the data is sensitive. The dilemma here is that they need the facilities of the network but they need them outside the building, and the Internet can provide these but the information is confidential.

This is an ideal candidate for an intranet – the executives can go to the company's website and then select the private area (or a more secure method is to have a separate URL that isn't advertised). The executives are authenticated in some way and then allowed access to the sensitive data contained in the site.

The name 'Intranet' is sometimes used to describe an 'internal' internet based upon files that are only open to users of the company's LAN. Although this is not exactly what is meant by the term intranet – because it is providing web facilities to a closed group – it can be regarded as an intranet.

Virtual private networks (VPNs)

Whilst the facilities intranets provide are extremely useful, there is a potential security risk in that the data can be 'eavesdropped' as it travels across the Internet. VPNs offer a solution to this by encrypting the data before it travels across the Internet. VPNs are set up by configuring the roaming machine as a VPN client, and a machine in the organisation as a VPN server (specialist hardware is available to act as a VPN server, but this task can also be undertaken by a Windows server operating system from Windows 2000 server onwards or a third party package).

Once configured, the roaming machine can contact the VPN server through the Internet in a conventional manner. Once connected, the VPN server and client go into a predetermined encryption mode and the data is sent between the two in an encrypted format. Once received by the VPN server, the data is decrypted and passed on to the organisational LAN (*Figure 1.10*). At this point, the data from the roaming machine has an identity inside the organisation, giving it access to the organisational LAN.

When sent back to the roaming client, the data passes through the VPN server where it is encrypted before being passed on to the Internet. Upon receipt, the client decrypts the data for presentation to the user. This is a standard feature of Windows from 2000 onwards and can be found in Network Connections (*see Windows Help*), although a specialist hardware solution is more robust.

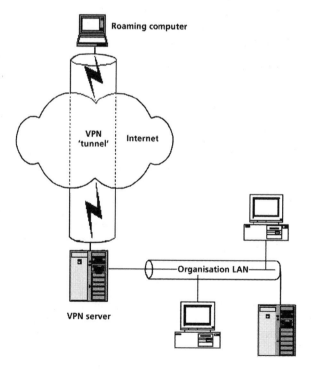

**Figure 1.10: Roaming machine contacting the
organisational LAN through a VPN**

Internet

The word 'Internet' is an abbreviation of internetwork – literally meaning a 'network of interconnected networks' – a definition that can be applied to many networks that could be part of the Internet or independent of it. Thus the Internet we all know (i.e. carrying web traffic) is effectively a worldwide internetwork of networks.

An example of an internetwork is a college or university that has a large number of network connections. Just as with a road, the more users who use it, the more congested it becomes and the slower everything runs. To ease such problems, the number of machines connected to a network is restricted and divided up into several, smaller networks. To provide the same functionality, the networks have to be 'internetworked' together, thus forming an Internet. In a large college or university, this internetwork is likely to comprise many smaller networks and can itself be connected to the Internet.

The Internet itself, when conceived, was a network of networks. Designed by the Advanced Research Projects Agency (ARPA) of the US Department of Defense (DoD) in the 1960s, the Internet was developed to span military bases across the world and to connect their networks. It needed to be robust and to be able to operate in the event of a nuclear strike. It was later extended to those organisations that worked with the DoD – e.g. universities and suppliers. As the Internet became more widely known, more and more institutions wanted to be connected (especially academic institutions), the number of connections on the Internet rose.

Until the early to mid-1990s, the Internet mainly carried text-based traffic (such as emails and files), although the standards for file transfer and remote login, etc. already existed. Any search was performed by a text-based utility called gopher. In the early 1990s, CERN introduced a hypertext system allowing text to be linked over the Internet (just as Microsoft Help files are linked). By 1994, the National Center for Supercomputer Applications (NCSA) enhanced this with its Mosaic browser, providing a graphical user interface (GUI) hypertext-based system. As anyone who has created a web page will know, the majority of a basic web page is text. Some elements are enclosed in tags (e.g. <p>), which are recognised by the browser and displayed in a particular way. This revolutionised the Internet and created the World Wide Web (www) that everyone wants to be a part of. However, the Internet is still the carrier of the web!

Extranets

Extranets are a popular discussion topic at the moment. An extranet essentially means extending access to an institution's network to its suppliers. Extranets are very popular because they can bring huge benefits. For example, a car manufacturer could extend access to its production network to its synchronous suppliers. By using this access, the suppliers could determine what cars were to be made that week and could ensure that they manufactured the correct components (e.g. seats) to go into the cars. Obviously, the seats would need to be the correct model and colour. In turn, by making their production schedule available to their own suppliers, the suppliers can ensure that the correct fabric is produced. In this example, none of the companies would need to hold much stock of finished goods but they can still fulfil the orders. By not holding stock they reduce storage and overall operating costs – hence the popularity of extranets.

KEY CONCEPT

The Internet is a network of networks and is a publicly accessible information resource. An intranet is essentially an internet for use only within an organisation. An extranet is effectively an intranet that is typically shared among an organisation's suppliers.

Section 4: Voice over IP

Organisations for a long time have had two distinct networks connecting up their offices – one for data and one for voice.

Obviously the cost of maintaining these two links is expensive and with the merging of telephone and data standards it has only been a matter of time before a solution became available.

Introduction

Voice over IP (VoIP) is a technology by which an organisations data network can be used to carry voice traffic as well as data. There are numerous pieces of software available, such as Microsoft's Netmeeting, which allow you to chat over the Internet. One of the key differences between these types of software and VoIP is quality.

VoIP is intended to replace the telephone service and as such must be at least as high a quality with key functions such as; reliability, ability to operate in the event of a power cut, switchboard functions, etc.

VoIP

VoIP requires special phones (*Figure 1.11*), which are essentially computers with a built in Ethernet switch. When the receiver is lifted or a button is pressed, the phone communicates over the network with a server such as Cisco's CallManager. When a number is dialled, CallManager looks up the telephone number and finds the IP address of the dialled phone (*see Chapter 3*). It then passes this back to the dialling phone, which can then communicate directly over the network. VoIP is extremely sensitive to delays and the organisational network must be configured to prioritise VoIP traffic.

The data packets required to send VoIP are small, and can usually be easily accommodated by the existing network. VoIP allows organisations to make significant savings by only having a data link between buildings and as such is likely to pay for itself within less than three years. VoIP also has many other features:

● Extension mobility – you can 'login' to your phone. Using this method no matter where you login, that phone will have your extension number.

● Features – IP phones are actually PCs and can be programmed using Java. Applications can be written for IP phones such as a register system in a school, further increasing the usefulness of the phone.

● Wireless IP phones can move around access points providing coverage right across an organisation, rather than within reach of a traditional cordless phone's base station.

● Relatively easy to relocate a phone.

The major disadvantage is the initial cost – the phones themselves are many times more expensive than a conventional phone, and they require specialist Ethernet switches (*see Chapter 6*) that can provide power over Ethernet cable.

Figure 1.11 A Cisco 7970G VoIP phone

> ### TIPS & ADVICE
>
> VoIP is fundamentally different from Internet Telephony – VoIP has a guaranteed quality of service (QoS), meaning that calls made with VoIP are normally slightly higher quality than those made with a conventional telephone.

Quick test

Identify the major differences between the three categories of networks.

Briefly discuss what is meant by the term VoIP.

Section 5: End of chapter assessment

Questions

1. Outline the major developments that led to today's networks.

2. Explain the differences and similarities between peer-to-peer and client server networks.

3. Explain what is meant by the terms LAN, MAN, WAN, PAN and VAN.

4. Explain what is meant by the term VoIP.

Answers

1. To answer this question, you need to review the development of networks from the early days, when computers had no real networks (single-stream systems) up to the introduction of local area networks. In your answer you should include local interactive terminals and remote access through both modem and leased lines. Remember that diagrams are important. If you can draw a diagram it makes your answer easier to mark (always a good ploy), and it shows the assessor you understand. The diagrams are relatively simple and drawing them serves as a prompt for you. At each stage you should also discuss the reasons why networking developed and the benefits each particular phase gave to the users of the network. Ideally, you should also discuss any weaknesses of the stage and relate these to the next stage of development to give a smooth flow.

2. As you progress through higher education the aim is to make you a reflective practitioner – someone who can review an idea or a concept critically. The earlier you learn this technique the better – it will allow you to pick up additional marks at Level 1 (HNC and Fd Level 1) and Level 2 (HND and Fd Level 2) because it is not expected there; instead, assessors expect descriptions or explanations – you can go one better! In answering this question you need to provide the assessor with a discussion of both the client/server network architecture and of the peer-to-peer network architecture. If you begin with the discussion of client/server architecture, you can highlight its composition, the benefits it has brought to organisations and any limiting factors (the major one being cost, of course). This will lead you smoothly into a discussion of peer-to-peer networks since these are meant to provide similar benefits to organisations, but at less cost.

   Again, diagrams may help illustrate your answer and will impress the assessor with your command of the subject. Diagrams allow assessors to see at a glance what the physical difference is between peer-to-peer and client/server networking. Extra marks will come from discussing limitations or problems with the architectures – for example, that Microsoft recommends no more than ten computers in a peer-to-peer network. Concluding the answer by discussing which network architecture is appropriate for an example organisation will demonstrate an understanding of the implementation of the subject and gain extra marks.

3. Again, an explanation and, again, diagrams can help with the explanation. The assessor wants you to demonstrate that you know of and understand the four major categories of networking:

    - LANs;
    - MANs;
    - WANs;
    - PANs.

    This is your chance to impress with the currency of your knowledge by illustrating that you also know of an emerging category called VANs. Don't spend too much time on VANs as the assessor may have a marking scheme based only on the four, but quote a website or an example (e.g. a train) that illustrates your point. A successful answer would list the four categories and then discuss the properties of each of the categories – the geographic area they cover, speed, costs, who administers, any involvement from telecomms providers, etc. Typical applications and uses of the category will help demonstrate you have the ability to apply the knowledge. Don't be afraid to quote a university or college campus, classroom or national/multinational company in the categories, as these are perfect textbook examples.

4. To answer this question you need to give a basic discussion of VoIP detailing what it is, what equipment is needed and what the advantages/disadvantages of this technology are. VoIP is a benefit or a use of networking so you shouldn't be asked too technical a question on it – unless you are studying a VoIP course!

Section 6: Further reading and research

Cisco Networking Academy Program (2004) CCNA 1 and 2 *Companion Guide* (3rd edn). Cisco Press. ISBN: 1 58713 50 1. Chapters 1 and 2.

www.bluetooth.com
www.usb.org

Chapter 2
The networked system

Chapter summary

Networked computer systems are part of almost every organisation in the western world. And not without good reason: networked computer systems allow organisations unparalleled access to their information irrespective of geographic location. They make communicating between different machine types possible and, when coupled with the Internet, make e-commerce possible.

Organisations are constantly looking for ways in which they can save money or gain a competitive advantage – networks offer the promise of both.

Learning outcomes

After studying this chapter you should aim to test your achievement of the following outcomes. You should be able to:

Outcome 1: Networked resources

Understand the essential components of any networked system and be able to identify these components. Question 1 at the end of this chapter will test your ability to do this.

Outcome 2: Facilities of a networked operating system

Understand the facilities and benefits a networked operating system (NOS) can provide to an organisation. Question 2 at the end of this chapter will test your ability to do this.

Outcome 3: Capacity issues

Understand that a network has limited bandwidth (capacity) and that applications that run on the network need to be both suitable and within the capacity of the network. Question 3 at the end of this chapter will test your ability to do this.

Outcome 4: Security implications

Understand that connecting a computer to a network will greatly increase the security risks and be aware of such risks. Question 4 at the end of this chapter will test your ability to do this.

Outcome 5: Licensing issues

Understand the licensing issues associated with networked software and be able to provide advice. Question 5 at the end of this chapter will test your ability to do this.

How will you be assessed on this?

This chapter is very much introductory – setting out the major components of networking and identifying the benefits and issues associated with their use. The ideal assessment in this case would be a case study of an organisation that wished to install a network. A case study would allow you to discuss all you have learnt from this chapter in a manner relevant to the organisation. It is therefore likely that such an assessment will be an assignment. The questions at the end of this chapter form such a case study.

Section 1: Networked resources

Computer networks are essential to most organisations and critical to a high number – that is to say, if the organisation was deprived of its network, it would no longer be able to carry out its mission. Such networks are considered 'mission critical'.

It might be thought that such mission critical networks would be restricted to large organisations, but this is not the case. A reasonably large taxi company whose bookings are stored on a computer system and dispatched by that system would consider its network as mission critical. If it was unable to access the server, it would be unable to dispatch the taxis; if it couldn't do that, it couldn't carry out its mission.

There are essential components to any networked system and this section explores these critical components.

Overview of network resources

From *Chapter 1* we know that a network provides a means by which two or more computers can communicate. It is desirable to have such communications as they allow the efficient sharing of files and printers and make possible such communications as the web and email. In short, they tie together data, communications, computing and file servers. They also provide a mechanism by which data can be transferred between differing machine types – for example, Apple MACs and PCs.

When considering resources, the best starting point is the computer itself: somehow the computer needs to be enabled to use the network. This is achieved by the installation of a Network Interface Card (or NIC). An NIC interfaces the computer's architecture with that of the network and facilitates connection between the two. Because of this, the NIC is said to be both network media dependent and computer hardware dependent. In short, the NIC you select needs to match both the internal architecture of the computer (e.g. PCI, ESIA, ISA) and the technology/media of the LAN (e.g. 100BaseT Ethernet). *Figure 2.1* shows a selection of NICs, whilst *Figure 2.2* shows the installation of an NIC. All computers that are to communicate over the network need to have NICs installed, most modern PCs have Ethernet NICs on board the system board.

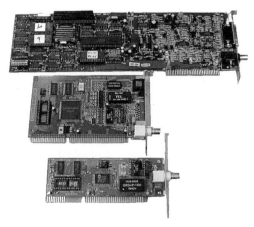

Figure 2.1: A selection of network interface cards (NICs)

Figure 2.2: The installation of a NIC

KEY CONCEPT

The NIC must match the computer architecture, LAN technology and media. For example, a 100BaseT PCI Ethernet card is meant for computers with a PCI slot and for Ethernet technology that runs over UTP cabling (*see Chapters 3 and 5*).

The computer is now electrically able to transfer data outside itself but doesn't have any form of connection with other computers and requires communications media. Most commonly, copper cables interconnect the machines. However, there is a variety of other media that are used in computer networking to carry the data – for example, fibre optic is used to carry light, and even air itself is used to carry radio waves (wireless LANs, Bluetooth) and light (infrared communication). To keep things simple we will look at a common medium – copper. *Figure 2.3* shows Unshielded Twisted Pair (UTP) cabling, which is the most common form of connection today (terminating in an RJ-45 plug).

Figure 2.3: The correctly made-up end of UTP cabling

The media needs to be connected to the computers that are being networked, which may require the use of networking devices such as a hub or switch (*Figure 2.4*) (for further information, *see Chapter 5*). Our computers are then able to communicate with the outside world and are physically connected together. The final requirement is the software itself! On a Microsoft Windows platform, two pieces of software are necessary:

- driver software for the NIC;
- Windows itself.

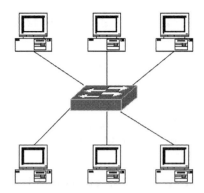

Figure 2.4: Computers networked using an Ethernet switch

As with most accessories purchased for a PC, NICs are shipped with a driver disk. The driver disk simply allows the computer to use (or 'drive') the hardware and needs to be installed before attempting to network the computer – otherwise the operating system won't be able to find the NIC! Since Windows for workgroups was launched in the mid-1990s the Windows operating system has had the ability to communicate over networks. The network settings can be found in the Control Panel (*see Figure 2.5*).

Figure 2.5: Control Panel settings; note the networking icon

Quick test

List the essential components of a networked operating system and briefly outline their purpose.

Section 2: Facilities of a networked operating system

Quite simply, networked operating systems (or NOSs) enable almost any make of computer to communicate with almost any other make of computer. Although this sounds relatively simple, it is not – and the power such simple communication provides to an organisation is tremendous. As things continue to 'become digital', digital representation can be effectively moved on a computer network. Thus, as the digital revolution continues, the products can be shipped by the network – making things possible that were never dreamt of.

Why are computer networks so popular?

Networking has, throughout its history, brought huge benefits to organisations. For example, the ability of early programmers to work online was immeasurable in terms of efficiency and effectiveness. Before the advent of PCs in the 1980s, computing was undertaken on either mini or mainframe computers. As these were hugely expensive, organisations with such machines needed to ensure maximum use was being made of them whilst the machines themselves were kept secure. The most effective way of achieving this was via remote access through the network. Thus, in local authorities and large companies throughout the world, the resources of the computer – processing power, disk storage, printing, etc. – were shared, providing maximum benefits for the cost.

In the early 1980s, IBM introduced the first PC, which was an instant success with organisations the world over. Processing power was brought to the desktop, as were files and printing devices. Having the files and printers local to a machine was, at first, a novelty – users were in charge of their own data, printing and processing power. Organisations very quickly realised that, although there were benefits to this approach, there were also drawbacks. Files, which needed to be shared, had to be swapped physically (sometimes referred to as 'sneakernet' – a term which comes from walking around with a disk); expensive printing resources had to be duplicated; and the organisation's data was decentralised, difficult to locate, access and back-up. Take, for example, the booking office taking bookings for a popular gig we looked at briefly in *Chapter 1*. The seating area (file) needs to be shared amongst everyone taking the bookings, otherwise over- or under-booking may occur. This cannot be effectively undertaken by sharing a floppy disk! As this example illustrates, the sharing of information in an organisation is critical. To most organisations, communication and the sharing of information are critical. A sales department may ask: 'Can production handle this extra order if we take it?' If production keep their data local, this will be difficult to find out and the order might be lost.

LANs were soon added to the PC platform providing a means where the users could have their processing power locally, but could share information and other resources such as expensive printers. The first LANs introduced to the PC environment were client/server LANs and, today, the majority still are. However, such are the benefits provided by LANs that smaller organisations have introduced peer-to-peer LANs to provide similar benefits. As LANs have evolved, so have the benefits they provide. Early LANs provided facilities for file and printer sharing. Today, LANs provide many more benefits to the organisation. For example:

- distributed processing (where the server can process, for example, a database query before returning the results to the client);
- email facilities and file transfer;
- remote backup;
- video conferencing;
- fax;

- shared applications, such as accounting and payroll systems (subject to licence terms);

- shared data;

- telephony services.

Using email as an example, few would argue that email has revolutionised communication. For example, in 2002, a fire at a chemical plant sent a toxic cloud over the north east. The university in which I work had one call from the police advising everyone to stay inside. Relaying this life-threatening information to 1500 employees was achieved in seconds using email. Staff could then inform students to stay inside.

Sharing information (such as working documents) with colleagues is difficult and time-consuming without email (the file would have to be copied to one disk per colleague and put in the internal post). It is much more effective to use email and simply attach the file. The network, therefore, also has to provide the translation between different machine types. Thus a Mac computer can send and receive emails to and from a PC, which is easier than sharing floppy disks (due to the different formats between MACs and PCs). The phrase 'information is power' is certainly true – the organisation that can share and access the information the quickest is likely to be the one that progresses the fastest. In every sense, networks provide an organisation with many ways of communicating more effectively. The fact that the cost of providing these facilities is relatively low means that the networks are providing low-cost/high-benefit solutions to an organisation – hence their popularity and continued growth.

KEY CONCEPT

Networking has brought many benefits to organisations, allowing them to realise huge savings. Such a positive cost-benefit has fuelled the development of networks. Organisations can almost always benefit from enhancing their networks.

Quick test

Identify the benefits networks bring to an organisation and, hence, why they are so popular.

Section 3: Capacity and performance issues

Computer networks bring enormous benefits to an organisation and, therefore, organisations often become critically dependent upon their networks. Unfortunately, computer networks do not have unlimited capacity, and it is important to realise that this can often be a limiting factor. This is particularly so when connecting externally, either via a WAN or the Internet. (*Chapter 7* covers capacity in more detail.)

Capacity limitations

Perhaps the single most limiting factor of a computer network is its capacity to carry data. Unfortunately, networks lag behind computer architectures in terms of the amount of information they can pass from point to point. This is due, in part, to networks providing serial as opposed to parallel transmission. It is also due to the fact that the network is shared amongst many computers, where the faster internal architecture of a computer is reserved for its own use.

It is often helpful to think of a computer network in terms of plumbing. No one would dream of supplying the water needs to a twenty-storey hotel from a garden hose! There obviously isn't enough capacity in a garden hose – it isn't big enough to let the required amount of water through and neither is the tap. If such a water supply was used, the water would slow to a trickle for each user, and the problem would become more acute during peak times – early morning and when many people wanted a bath (high-volume users). In fact, if the water was fed from the bottom of the building it is likely that, during peak times, only the bottom floor would have a supply. This is because there is insufficient capacity. We can substitute the hotel for a computer LAN (say, 30 stations) and the garden hose for the LAN technology. If we have 10Base2 (see Chapter 5), we have a maximum of 7 Mbps (technically 10Base2 has a theoretical maximum of 10 Mbps but in practice it's nearer 7 Mbps) shared amongst every user of the LAN. Thus in every second we can transfer a maximum of 7 Mbps for all computers. To take an example, poor-quality video is approximately 10 MB per minute: 10 MB x 8 = 80 Mbits. 80 Mb/60 secs tells us that each machine requires 1.34 Mbits per second (Mbps) capacity to show the video over a LAN. If we have 30 machines, there is no way the LAN can cope.

> ### TIPS & ADVICE
> It is important to remember that data is measured in megabytes (MB) and networks work in megabits (Mb). To convert you need to multiply by MB by 8.

When considering placing an application on the LAN, the effects of doing so must be taken into account. If the LAN in our example was mission critical, by adding the video we would slow the information on the LAN to a trickle – which would mean the organisation would be unable to carry out its mission. This could seriously damage the organisation. For a store like Argos at Christmas, if an employee chose to watch a video over the LAN, slowing it to a trickle, it might well take 30 minutes to serve each customer! The one thing that is certain about bandwidth is that we can never have enough. An organisation's requirements will constantly grow, just as LAN capacity will grow.

> ### KEY CONCEPT
> Networks don't have unlimited capacity. When introducing applications or data to the LAN or making changes, we must ensure that the LAN can cope with the new load (see Chapter 7).

Quick test

Describe briefly what is meant by the term 'bandwidth'. Discuss why it is important to assess bandwidth and its impact when considering installing a networked application.

Section 4: Security implications

Whilst computer networks undoubtedly provide unparalleled access to information, they can also provide it to prying eyes. As soon as information is networked, it is shared with people we want to share it with and those we don't want to share it with. Hence the need for security measures. (Security is given fuller treatment in Chapters 8, and 12.)

Security implications

Information security is often as paramount for commercial organisations as it is for military organisations. Companies have commercially-sensitive information as well as obligations under such legislation as the Data Protection Act 1984 to keep it secure. Before the widespread use of computers, information security was provided by rugged filing cabinets, perhaps a security guard and, usually, a personnel-screening system. The aim was simple – to limit access to sensitive information. Unauthorised access to such information could be damaging to the company. Consider a car dealership – access to customer lists would be very helpful to other dealers.

Before the widespread use of computers, it was relatively easy to spot someone stealing information – long periods spent at the photocopier and carrying large boxes of paper out of the building. The widespread use of computers makes it much easier to steal information. By using a DAT cartridge it is possible to steal 72 GB of data on a cartridge small enough to fit into a shirt pocket (to put 72 GB in context – the entire *Encyclopaedia Britannica* is around 1 GB!). Essentially, anyone connected to the corporate network has access to the information held on its computers and also travelling across the network. Organisations need to take steps to protect the contents of their servers and other computers. Access to servers should be via a password only, and users should be given the minimum access rights necessary for them to carry out their work. Computers (including PCs) that are connected to a corporate network should be reviewed to ensure that only the files and directories that need to be shared are shared and that all others are protected. Again, access to shared drives should be via a password only.

KEY CONCEPT

Security should be paramount. To ignore security is to risk the organisation's entire existence – it cannot be treated as piecemeal. All organisations must take a professional approach to computer security.

Quick test

Briefly discuss why security is a vitally important issue with reference to information held on a network.

Section 5: Licensing issues

Breaking licence agreements is a civil offence, as is a breach of copyright or copying software. Software piracy is a serious issue and is reported to be costing the software industry billions of dollars each year. In 1984, the British Computer Society's Copyright Committee established the Federation Against Software Theft (or FAST). The aim of FAST is to safeguard software and, contrary to popular belief, the organisation represents both users and software producers. FAST can assist in identifying and prosecuting organisations or individuals who copy or use copied software or who breach licence agreements. Unauthorised copying of software and breaches of a software licence are serious crimes and there can be severe penalties for those caught. The network manager is often the one who is nominated to oversee an organisation's licence agreements, and such managers must understand licensing issues fully.

Licensing issues

Discussion of software licensing has necessarily been limited here. Network managers must ensure they understand their position fully and the wider issues involved. Before computer networks, licensing issues were relatively simple – a licence was bought for every machine the software was to be installed upon. If an organisation had 25 machines but only 10 were in use at any one time, it still needed 25 copies of the software or one per CPU. With the advent of computer networks, software could be held centrally and downloaded to a machine when required. Software manufacturers realised this and released appropriately designed networked versions of their software. Central to these licences is the issue of concurrency. Thus, a ten-user licence of networked software usually means a maximum of ten machines can be using that software at one time. When an eleventh user downloads and runs the software, this is a breach of the licence agreement. Some manufacturers include the word 'normally' in the licence agreement: 'the number of users of the software will normally not exceed x'. The intention here is that, in exceptional circumstances, they would not be averse to more users than the licence permits, although there will be restrictions. An example of this could be the student records system in your institution. Normally it may only have eight users but, during times of enrolment extra staff may be needed to cope. This term, however, does not apply to all software and its meaning should be checked with the manufacturers.

Some argue that a user logging into a network and starting a piece of networked software may be unaware that the maximum number of licences have been used and that it is the software itself that should enforce the licence agreement. The argument about the user logging in is, however, valid – an organisation should know how many people are likely to be using a piece of software at one time. For example, if a university has three classes of 25 students using Microsoft Office, it should know it needs 75 licences. Some software does, on the other hand, enforce the licensing agreement through a licence meter. This works by the software either refusing to start if the maximum number of licences has been reached or – more cruelly – logging out the user who has been connected for the longest period of time. Whilst the use of a meter sounds good, in practice it can be problematic. If a machine crashes whilst using the software it may not release the licence and, when restarted, may consume another licence. Eventually, this could lead to the situation where all the licences have been consumed through faults and so no one can use the software. This would obviously lead to frustration and to increased technical support costs.

Quick test

Briefly discuss the main issues concerning software licensing.

KEY CONCEPT

An organisation must ensure it has sufficient software licences for the software in use. In the case of operating systems this will usually mean one licence per computer (as all computers need an operating system). Other software may be available in a networked version. An organisation should also ensure that the maximum number of concurrent users allowed under the licence agreements is never exceeded. Exceeding the licence agreement may result in prosecution, and the authorities take a serious view of such cases.

Software licences and agreements do change over time, so remember to keep abreast.

Section 6: End of chapter assessment

Questions

1. You have been approached by a local charity that wishes to network their office. It has limited funds and has asked you to identify the minimum resources it would need to network its office. It currently runs donated copies of Windows 98.

2. The charity is aiming to help the unemployed over-fifties to get to grips with computing in the hope they can find employment. Typically, it intends to train ten students at a time in the use of word processors. The charity also has a small administration team of three. Two of the team typically use Microsoft Word and Access on a daily basis, handling confidential files on the charity's students and producing references for employment. A further administrator uses Excel. The functions this team provide can be considered mission critical. As the charity does not have sufficient printing resources, it would like the administration team to be connected to the network. Outline the benefits a network would offer the charity.

3. The founder of the charity has recently acquired a high quality 1.5 GB AVI video which, over a period of 15 minutes, introduces the trainees to the benefits of word processing and many of the techniques they need. She feels that the class can use the video throughout the lesson rather than having formal instruction. As the charity will be networked, she feels that delivery of the video over the network will be ideal and has sought your advice.

4. The charity has also asked your advice on the security implications of connecting the administrative staff to the teaching network.

5. The charity has a ten-user licence for Microsoft Word, which is currently used by two administrators. It wishes to use the same licence for the classes it intends to teach and has asked for your advice on the licensing issues of such a move.

Answers

The questions above are all inter-related and are based upon a small case study. This is deliberate as it is likely that assessment of such topics will be in this form. Thus the answers below are likely to form subsections of your overall answer. In practice, the case study would go into far greater detail and would be tied in with capacity planning covered in *Chapter 7*.

1. To answer this question, you need to pick up on the key facts – the organisation is a charity and has limited funds. It is seeking your advice on the minimum resources it needs to get its network operational. Obviously there are two sides to this question, as it is meant to test your academic knowledge – the assessor is not just looking for a shopping list, but for a list of items the charity requires together with an **explanation** of why it needs them and some form of explanation of what the items actually do/a justification of why they are needed. Don't forget: for a network to be successful, you need both hardware and software and the software they have would appear to support their requirements.

2. This question is asking you to outline the benefits a computer network would bring to the charity. Although this is a case study, there is considerable scope in the benefits it can provide. Again, don't forget that the assessor isn't simply looking for a list of benefits: he or she is looking to see that you understand the benefits (shown through discussion) and that the benefits you propose are realistic and achievable within the charity's limited budget.

3. This question is about managing the expectations of the end-user. Networks are useful and do provide enormous benefits, but they have limited bandwidth. In this example the founder of the charity has great expectations of the network, which it won't be able to deliver inside of her limited budget (assuming the charity will install a 10 or 100 Mbps Ethernet network – *see Chapter 5*). You need to discuss the fact that networks have limited bandwidth and advise her on what is and is not realistic.

4. Although this question is simple enough, the answer is more complex and, as usual in such an assessment, some of the clues are hidden elsewhere. If you review the earlier questions, you will see what information is actually being held and processed on the computers connected to the network. You need to outline to the charity the security implications of what it intends to do. Again, a list isn't required – the assessor is after evidence of thought and wants to see discussion of the issues as well as guidance for the charity.

5. The answer to this question centres on software licensing issues. To answer it you need to provide a general discussion of the software licensing issues and relate this to the case of the charity. It has a networked ten-user licence for Microsoft Word, but it is likely that, at peak times, it will exceed this licence. You need to inform the charity of the implications of this.

Section 7: Further reading and research

Cisco Networking Academy Program (2004) *CCNA 1 and 2 Companion Guide* (2nd edn). Cisco Press. ISBN: 1 58713 150 1. Chapters 1 and 2.

Cisco Networking Academy Program (2003) *CCNA 3 and 4 Companion Guide* (2nd edn). Cisco Press. ISBN: 1 58713 113 7. Chapter 18.

Chapter 3
Fundamentals of networks

Chapter summary

This chapter provides an introduction to computer networks and networking. When studying computer networking, it is important to understand that networking has evolved, and will continue to evolve, as the technology becomes available, and that the use to which the technology is being put and can be put will also evolve. A computer network can be categorised according to, for example, the geographical area it covers or by the access it provides to the outside world.

Learning outcomes

After studying this chapter you should aim to test your achievement of the following outcomes. You should be able to:

Outcome 1: Network basics

Understand the basics of computer networking and be familiar with some of the terms. Question 1 at the end of this chapter will test your ability to do this.

Outcome 2: Network topologies

Describe the common network topologies and be able to identify each. Question 2 at the end of this chapter will test your ability to do this.

Outcome 3: Network addressing

Understand the basics of network addressing and be able to discuss the addressing formats. Question 3 at the end of this chapter will test your ability to do this.

How will you be assessed on this?

The topics covered in this chapter form the fundamental principles of networking – how data is encoded, the different topologies and logical/physical addressing mechanisms. The most popular form of assessment for such topics is by examination or time-constrained test (TCT). The questions at the end of this chapter provide you with sample questions that may well be asked in such assessments.

Section 1: Understanding network basics

Computer networking is subject to the laws of physics, and therefore a basic understanding of the physics of networking will aid understanding. The laws of physics also govern the speed and development of networking. This section introduces some of the basic physics that impact on networking. It assumes that you understand binary – that binary is the basis of all data held and transmitted by a computer, digital signals, analogue signals and digital-to-analogue conversion. If this is not the case, it is recommended you consult a book on computer architectures to pick up these basics before proceeding.

Encoding

Computer networking is about moving data (in the form of bits) along some sort of transmission media (most commonly, a piece of wire). For transmission, the data needs to be encoded into a electrical voltage that can then be carried by the wire.

> **TIPS & ADVICE**
>
> Although it might seem odd, a great deal can be gleaned from comparing networking to plumbing. Here, how a wire carries data (represented by a voltage) is likened to a pipe carrying water.

Figure 3.1 shows data encoding using +12 v to represent a 0 and 12 v to represent a 1. It is common usage to employ two voltages to differentiate a no signal state from a signal state. Thus, if the sender is at the right and the receiver at the left, the data 0101010 is being transmitted.

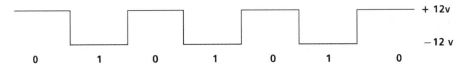

Figure 3.1: Data encoding
(diagram courtesy of Professor Peter Hodson, University of Glamorgan)

Any good computer architecture book will detail how alphanumeric characters are encoded using an encoding mechanism such as the American Standard Code for Information Interchange (ASCII).

Circuits

To carry data a circuit is required. In most cases a circuit comprises two wires. Consider *Figure 3.2*, which is a simple torch circuit. Here, when the switch is closed, the electrons move, providing electricity to the bulb, which lights up. Opening the switch stops the flow of electrons and the light goes out. This circuit could be used to represent basic binary digits (either 1 (on) or 0 (off)).

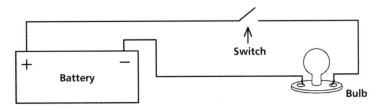

Figure 3.2: Simple torch circuit

Networking also needs complete circuits – we call the cables the 'signal' and the signal 'ground'. As can be seen from *Figure 3.1*, determining the height of the signal (the voltage) accurately is of crucial importance. The signal wire carries the signal whilst the signal ground completes the circuit and allows the height of the signal to be determined. In practice, networks often use multiple voltage levels to represent many bit patterns. For example, by using four voltages we can encode two bits to each voltage, which allows transmission of twice as much data by each voltage level:

Voltage 1	00
Voltage 2	01
Voltage 3	10
Voltage 4	11

Three types of circuits are commonly used in networking:

- simplex – can carry signals in one direction only (e.g. a one-way street or a public address system);

- half duplex – can carry signals in both directions, but only one direction at a time (e.g. a narrow bridge where traffic from only one direction can cross at a time – under traffic light control or a walkie talkie);

- full duplex – carries signals in both directions simultaneously (e.g. dual carriage way or a telephone).

TIPS & ADVICE

You must understand these three types of circuits, as they are often referred to in a range of networking situations.

Signal problems

Electrical signals are susceptible to a wide range of interference. For example, as the signal travels along the wire it loses some of its strength and arrives at the destination weaker (a lower voltage), which makes it more difficult to determine how it was originally encoded – hence the big difference in the voltage levels used to represent a 0 and a 1. This loss of strength is known as **attenuation** and limits the distance a signal can travel without being amplified or regenerated. Attenuation can be addressed in analogue networks by amplifying the signal or, in digital networks, by repeating or regenerating the signal. Repeating is preferable as the signal generated by repeating is a perfect signal like the original, whereas amplifying also amplifies noise – similar to the quality difference between a DVD (digital) and a video (analogue).

TIPS & ADVICE

Assessors quite like the topic of sources of error as an examination question.

The following is a summary of the common sources of error:

- **Attenuation**   As the signal travels along the cable it becomes weaker. On long-distance runs, unless it is aided, the signal received can be too weak to use. On 100BaseT Ethernet, it is recommended that the cable lengths be no more than 100 m.

- **Impulse noise**   Sometimes known as electromagnetic interference (EMI), electrical signals given off by some electrical devices (e.g. fluorescent lights and electrical motors) can cause severe degradation to the signal or even destroy it. Lightning is also a cause of impulse noise. Care should be taken when routing the network cable to avoid close contact with such devices.

- **Thermal noise**   Thermal noise is the interference that comes from the cable itself – the distortion caused by moving the electrons. Very little can be done to address this.

- **Crosstalk**   Crosstalk is when two or more pairs of cables lying near each other interfere with the signals on the other cable. This used to be common on older telephone networks where you could hear someone else's conversation if you were quiet. Crosstalk can be largely eliminated by twisting the two wires in the circuit together (hence twisted pair cabling).

- **Intermodulation noise**   Similar to crosstalk except that, here, the signals which interfere are being transmitted on the same cable (*see Broadband/baseband* *below*). A good example of this in the UK is Channel 5 TV, which is transmitted on a frequency used by most video recorders – if the video and Channel 5 are switched on together they often interfere with each other. This problem can be addressed by altering the frequencies used for transmission.

- **Radiation**   Just as atmospheric conditions interfere with TV signals, they can also interfere with computer networks and telephone networks. Thankfully, such interference is rare and can be addressed by using shielded cabling.

- **Radio frequency interference** (RFI)   RFI is interference caused by devices emitting radio signals in the proximity of the network cable. Again, electric motors and fluorescent lights can be a source of this. Other sources include mobile phones and other devices that transmit radio signals. Reduction of such interference is identical to impulse noise.

- **Signal reflection**   If a network cable is not terminated correctly, the transmitted signal is reflected back from the open end of the cable and interferes with the remainder of the signal and others that follow. This was a particular problem with 10Base2 and 10Base5 networks.

Electrostatic discharge (ESD)

Often referred to simply as 'static' or 'static electricity', ESD is caused by the electrons becoming loosened and staying in one place, where they look for an opportunity to 'jump' to a conductor. ESD is the shock we feel when we have built up a charge from, for example, dragging our feet on a nylon carpet and then touching something – perhaps a metal stair bannister. Other than a shock, it is usually harmless to human beings, but to sensitive electronic components, such as those found inside a computer or networking devices, it can be fatal. ESD can be as high as 40,000 volts, which can wreak havoc on a 5-volt computer circuit.

Broadband/baseband

A TV aerial cable carries many channels (e.g. BBC1 and ITV1). Although there is only one piece of cable the companies are able to transmit the channels using discrete frequencies – a different frequency for each channel. Technically, this is known as **broadband signalling**.

Computer networks can operate in a similar fashion – the available frequency range of the cable can be divided up and used to transmit different signals. Broadband services from telecommunications companies use this concept – one channel for Internet access and other, separate channels for telephones and (sometimes) fax. Thus a device needs to be employed at the socket to divide the signals.

Alternatively, a signal can occupy the entire frequency range, which is known as **baseband signalling**. This allows the signal to use all the frequency range available on the cable and, hence, it has a higher throughput (more bandwidth). Ethernet uses this principle.

Packets

Data to be transmitted across the network is broken down into chunks known as **packets**. There are two main reasons for breaking the data down into chunks. To

- reduce the amount of data lost to noise; and
- ensure fair access to the medium.

> **TIPS & ADVICE**
>
> Remember, data is measured in megabytes (MB) and data on a network is measured in megabits (Mb).

Let's imagine we need to transmit 2 MB of data – 2 x 8 gives us 16 Mb. Let's assume that, on average, the network can transmit only 2 Mb before an error occurs. Thus we could never transmit the data as a 16 Mb entity successfully – each transmission will be corrupted by an error and require retransmission. If we break the data into packets of, say, 0.5 Mb each, on average we will successfully transmit three packets before an error occurs, requiring only 0.5 Mb to be retransmitted. By reducing the size of the packet further, we can prevent even more data loss. However, as each packet needs to contain the sender and receiver addresses and some mechanism for detecting errors, if we reduce the packet size too much these overheads will also reduce performance. For this and other reasons, packet size is fixed by network technology designers and cannot be altered by the user.

Breaking data into packets also provides a fairer way of sharing the medium – users each send a packet at a time rather than 'hogging' the medium until their transmission is over.

Error detection/correction

We cannot prevent errors from occurring in data transmission and it is imperative we detect all errors, since data with an error must not be used – consider a spreadsheet with financial information – if an error has occurred we don't know that the amounts are correct and so it is unsafe to use the data. You will most likely have studied parity as an error detection method in the past. Parity is one method of error detection but it is not accurate enough for today's networks because it does not detect all errors. Instead, we use Cyclic Redundancy Checks (CRCs) based on 32 bit polynomials to detect errors. All that needs to be known is that they detect 99.997% of all errors and that correction requires the data to be retransmitted.

Quick test

1. Briefly describe how data can be sent over a computer network. Your answer should include encoding.

2. Describe the differences between full duplex, half duplex and simplex circuits.

3. Briefly describe the kinds of interference that can occur in computer networks and how these can be addressed.

Section 2: Network topologies

The words 'technology' and 'topology' are often used when discussing networks, and it is important to clarify these terms. Technologies are the hardware devices and their operation, whereas topology is the physical shape of the network. Different technologies require different topologies. In this section, the differing topologies available for computer networks are discussed, and the differences between logical and physical topology are distinguished.

> **TIPS & ADVICE**
>
> Naming and drawing diagrams of various networking topologies is a popular type of examination question. Examiners may also ask you to discuss which topologies support a networking technology (*see Chapter 5*).

Early star networks

In *Chapter 1*, we discussed the ways that local interactive terminals were connected to the mainframe computer – each had its own cable running back to the central computer forming a star pattern (the star network – *see Figure 3.3*).

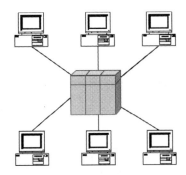

Figure 3.3: An early star network

Such cabling resulted in hundreds of cables descending upon the main computer and was costly in terms of cable and labour. Organisations often encountered problems in handling the sheer volume of cables, and relocating the central computer was a major issue.

The advantages of this type of topology, on the other hand, are:

- **robustness** – a cable break will only affect one machine;

- **performance** – each terminal has a dedicated cable.

RS232-C connectors (*Figure 3.4*) are the standard connectors used here (known as D.25). The cable used is twisted pair (*see Figure 3.19*).

Figure 3.4: D.25 serial connector

Point-to-point network

The point-to-point network is the simplest of all topologies. In the point-to-point topology (*Figure 3.5*), two computers are connected together via a physical wire. It is a network because it has networking hardware and software to facilitate the exchange of information. However, normally the overheads of a two-station network are greater than the benefits. Costing less than £30 at early 2005 prices (when based on Ethernet technology using a crossover cable and 10BaseT – *see Chapter 5*), this topology is useful in small organisations or the home where two computers perhaps share costly resources, such as a colour laser printer, or to facilitate file transfer.

Figure 3.5: Point-to-point network

Bus network

The bus network (*Figure 3.6*) used to be very common and was used by a number of technologies – most notably, Ethernet. In this topology, a central 'backbone' cable spans the area and computers 'tap' into this backbone for their connection. In a bus network, the communications medium is shared between the computers attached to it. The standard connector used in this type of network was the British Naval Connector (BNC) (*Figure 3.8*). The cable used was co-axial cable (similar to that used by TV aerials and cable TV) (*Figure 3.9*).

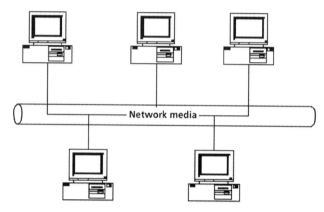

Figure 3.6: Bus network

The advantages of a bus network include the following:

● It is easy and inexpensive to install.

● It is easy to add further devices by tapping into the wire (avoiding the costs of expensive recabling).

● Bandwidth was higher than early star networks.

● Facilitates communication with the interconnected device without going through the central computer.

The disadvantages included the following:

● The media was shared – therefore there was contention for access that required an algorithm to ensure fairness.

● Data was sent in a broadcast fashion, meaning that all computers could 'see' the information – a security weakness.

● A cable break on the main bus cable took down the entire network.

● Although the cable was higher capacity, it was shared amongst many more users. As network traffic increased, capacity became an issue.

This kind of topology was popular (along with ring and tree networks) from the mid-1980s until around 1992, when the volume of network traffic started to increase dramatically and performance became an issue.

For cabling and connectors, *see tree network below*.

Tree network

It is possible to connect bus networks together to form a bus network that has branches with other bus networks. Such a topology is known as a **tree network** (*Figure 3.7*). As it is essentially a bus network, a tree network has the same advantages and disadvantages as a standard bus network. The devices used at the joints are known as **hubs** and are a specialist piece of hardware. The standard connector used in this type of network was the British Naval Connector (BNC) (*Figure 3.8*). The cable used was co-axial cable (similar to that used by TV aerials and cable TV) (*Figure 3.9*).

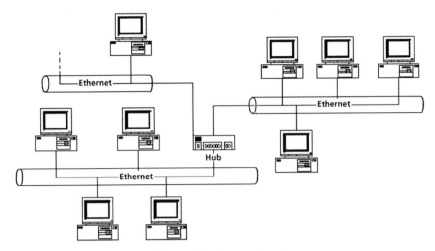

Figure 3.7: Tree network

Figure 3.8: British naval connector (BNC)

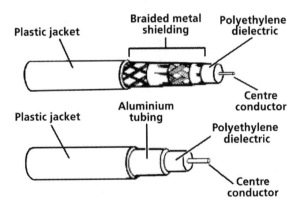

Figure 3.9: Coaxial cable
(diagram courtesy of Professor Peter Hodson, University of Glamorgan)

Ring network

In the ring topology (*Figure 3.10*), computers are connected to one another in a circular fashion and therefore form a ring. Although several companies and several implementations were involved, the two most notable were the Cambridge ring (developed in Cambridge University and used extensively by Acorn in the BBC microcomputer series) and the Token Ring (developed and used extensively by IBM). The dominant network in this topology was IBM's Token Ring network.

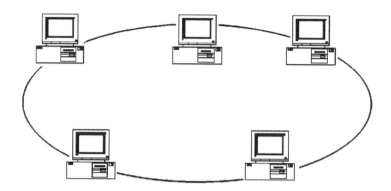

Figure 3.10: Ring network

The advantages of the ring topology are as follows:

- robustness – there are two links to each PC;
- in the case of Token Ring, higher capacity than 10Base2, 5 or T Ethernet;
- a fairer method of access than standard Ethernet (*see Chapter 5*).

The major disadvantage was cost. As the equipment used in the topology was IBM propriety technology (which had a royalty fee attached to it), it was substantially more expensive than bus networks. Eventually, Ethernet gained the lion's share of the market (due to costs) and later versions of Ethernet outstripped the Token Ring's capacity.

Star with logical ring

Occasionally, ring networks (especially IBM's Token Ring) appear to be a star network (*Figure 3.11*) as they run to a piece of hardware called a multistation access unit (MAU). This essentially connects all the computers together and gives the network a star appearance. However, the network is still very much a ring and operates as such.

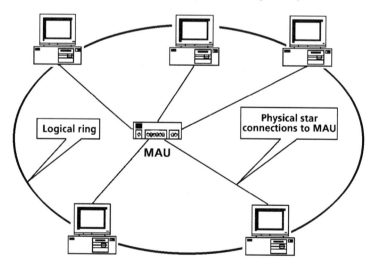

Figure 3.11: Logical ring

Connectors used in the IBM Token Ring are a proprietary technology (*Figure 3.12*), although most are now RJ-45. The cable used was shielded twisted pair (*Figure 3.13*). Shielded RJ-45 connectors are also commonly used with this technology (*Figure 3.14*) – note the metal sides to the RJ-45.

Figure 3.12: Typical Token Ring connectors

Figure 3.13: STP cabling
(diagram courtesy of Peter Hodson, University of Glamorgan)

Figure 3.14: STP RJ-45 connector (note the metal grounding)

Mesh network

The final topology is the mesh network (*Figure 3.15*). With a mesh network, a number of connections exist between machines and, in order to get from one machine to another, a route must be established. Mesh networks are complex and are designed to provide resilience in the event of a cable break. A mesh network can be either full or partial. In the case of a full mesh network, every node is directly connected to every other node – there is more than one route to every PC or network in the mesh. As its name suggests, a partial mesh network is not complete (*Figure 3.15* shows a full mesh network). The Internet itself is a mesh network, as part of its original design specification was resilience. The major advantage of mesh networks is resilience, and the major disadvantages are cost and complexity. Mesh networks are almost always WAN links and, therefore, the cabling is provided by the service provider. A typical connector (V.35) is shown in *Figure 3.16*.

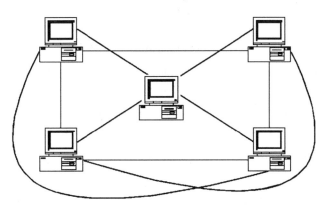

Figure 3.15: Full mesh network

Figure 3.16: Typical WAN serial connector (V.35)

Structured cabling solutions/modern star

Modern organisations experience a great deal of change during their lifetimes and have high demands for networks in terms of capacity and reliability. The original star network offered capacity that was dedicated to a terminal and that was extremely robust. Because of these advantages, the star network has been developed further and remains the preferred solution for modern cabling. A modern star network (see *Figure 3.17*) has, at its centre, a wiring closet to which all communications points (telephone sockets, computer sockets, etc.) on that floor are connected. Inside the wiring closet, each connection terminates in a patch panel which can then be connected to a service using a patch lead. Services would typically include different computer networks, telephone services and perhaps ISDN lines.

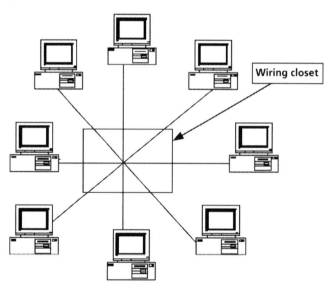

Figure 3.17: Modern star network

Known as a structured cabling solution, this is the recommended wiring structure for new installations, each installation requiring one wiring closet per 1000 m² floor space interconnected by cable (usually fibre), known as backbone cabling. Structured cabling specifications require a minimum of two connection points to be installed per user and provide a very flexible communications solution. *Figure 3.18* shows a typical structured cabling solution. The PC is connected through an interface card (*see Chapter 5*) via a 'drop cable' to the floor socket. This is connected directly to the patch panel in the wiring closet. A patch lead then 'patches' the required service from the service point to the patch panel. In this case, the service is an Ethernet network. The standards for structured cabling recommend that Category 5, or higher, unshielded twisted pair (UTP) cabling (*Figure 3.19*) is used throughout the installation, terminated by RJ-45 plugs (*Figure 3.20*) and sockets.

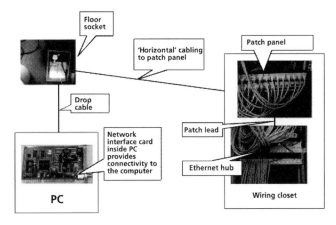

Figure 3.18: Typical structured cabling

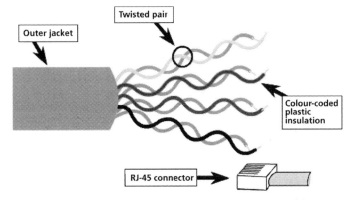

Figure 3.19: UTP cabling (diagram courtesy of Cisco Systems Inc.)

Figure 3.20: RJ-45 connector

TIPS & ADVICE

Structured cabling is now the standard in almost all new installations.

KEY CONCEPT

It is important to be able to remember the various topologies and to be able to draw these topologies.

Technologies

As well as having a physical shape, networks also need equipment in order for them to operate – for example, a network interface card (NIC), hub, etc. The equipment to support a network is known collectively as the technology (examples being Ethernet and Token Ring). The most popular technologies are discussed in detail in *Chapter 5.*

Quick test

1. Name the most common network topologies and discuss the differences between them.

2. For each of the topologies given, list any advantages/disadvantages.

Section 3: Network addressing and protocols

Computer networking is a complex business and requires rules to govern the communication. Such rules are known as protocols and are critical to computer networking. Most crucial of all is the open systems interconnection (OSI) seven-layer model for computer communication, which defines standards and protocols that are used extensively in the networking industry today.

Protocols

Computer communications are extremely complex, and there are many parameters that must be agreed before communication can take place. What was needed, therefore, was a standard (or protocol) for communication between computers. In other areas, this problem has been resolved by breaking down one large, complex problem into several smaller ones – for instance, with personal CD players the headphones jack is a standard 3.5 mm, therefore, any headphones can be used; it can play any audio-compatible CD; standard battery compartment means any make of batteries can be used; and, if the player has a mains adaptor, it can be plugged into any mains outlet that fits the adapter. This is because tight standards have been set that govern the production of all the pieces of equipment.

The same is true with networking: standards for networks were established and a model devised. This model, known as the Open Systems Interconnection (OSI) seven-layer model, was devised by members of ISO (the International Standards Organisation). The layers of the OSI seven-layer model are shown in *Figure 3.21*, and the model is discussed in detail in *Chapter 4*. Prior to the model (which was devised in the early 1980s), vendors tended to produce proprietary network solutions, which reduced the end-user's choice and limited the connectivity of the machine.

Application
Presentation
Session
Transport
Network
Datalink
Physical

Figure 3.21: The ISO seven-layer model

The benefits the layered model brings are as follows:

- It breaks network communication down into smaller simpler parts that are easier to develop.

- It facilitates the standardisation of network components to allow multi-vendor development and support.

- It allows different types of hardware and software to communicate with each other.

- It prevents changes in one layer from affecting the other layers so that layer technologies can be developed more quickly.

- It makes networks easier to learn.

Whilst the seven-layer model brings many benefits, it has several disadvantages:

- Redundant functions and facilities are retained.

- Simple communication is made over-complicated because of structure overheads.

- The structure overheads reduce the overall performance.

TIPS & ADVICE

Apart from their importance in the real world of networking, the benefits and disadvantages of layered approaches to networking is a very common question in TCTs.

Logical and physical addressing

Devices on a network must be able to communicate directly with one another and must be uniquely identified. Communication can then take place in a way similar to the postal system: the sender addresses an envelope or package to a recipient (including a return address). The postal system examines the recipient's address and forwards the package as appropriate. This may involve the package being forwarded to another postal network or sorting office before being delivered to the recipient.

Computer networks operate on an almost identical principle. Each machine on the network has an address to which data can be forwarded. In order to reach its recipient, the package may have to cross multiple networks before it is delivered. On a computer, there are two possible addressing mechanisms:

- physical; and

- logical.

Physical addressing (also known as layer two addressing as it occurs in layer two of the OSI model) mechanisms are used internally within an organisation. They use an address that is hardcoded on to the Media Access Control unit (MAC) – usually part of the networking card (i.e. the NIC). With Ethernet networks, this is either a 16 or 48 bit field (usually 48 bit) that is unique across the world. Burnt into ROM (on the NIC) and unable to be changed, the first half of the address identifies the manufacturer; the second half is the serial number within the manufacturer's ID. Thus replacing a card will change the MAC address. Whilst this is acceptable for local area networks where the address is circulated as the machine interacts, it would clearly be impossible to know the physical address of every machine in the world (and to keep that list up to date!). Thus another mechanism for addressing machines globally is needed – logical.

Logical addressing is used for three main reasons. To:

1. overcome the problem of a card change;

2. allow the demarcation of networks;

3. provide a structure to the addressing scheme.

The best analogy that can be drawn to logical addressing is the telephone network. If you purchased a phone and the serial number of that phone was your phone number, each time you changed the phone you would need to notify all your friends of your new number – something that is clearly undesirable. Also, as phones could be located anywhere in the world, when friends call you , the telephone network would have to try every phone in the world to find out if it was yours – a huge waste of resources. Instead, the telephone network is structured. For example, if you were to ring the University of Sunderland helpline from outside the UK, you would dial the following number:

00 44 191 5153000

The 00 routes the call from the local telephone exchange to an international one; the 44 routes the call to the UK; the 191 to the north east of England; the 515 to the University of Sunderland; and the 3000 is the number of the student helpline. This structure allows the telephone network to make much better use of its resources, and it allows demarcation of telephone networks – once the call has left one country/service provider it is the responsibility of another. Also, you can change your phone at will without having to notify your friends because your telephone number remains the same.

Logical addressing for networks is very similar. The most popular logical addressing mechanism is that used on the Internet – Internet Protocol (IP) addressing. With IP addressing, an organisation is issued a block of IP addresses from its Internet Service Provider (ISP), which is issued these by the Network Information Center in the USA, or their agents (early in Internet development, the Network Information Center would issue blocks of numbers, known as licences, directly to large organisations – *see below*). These numbers are 4 byte dotted decimal. For example:

157.228.102.1

KEY CONCEPT

We need to use logical addressing to provide a means by which we can structure traffic on the Internet and maintain independence from the MAC address.

Computers are thus grouped under the organisation's or ISP's network address, which are issued in licenses. Although these numbers are dotted decimal, they are actually a decimal representation of eight binary digits (a byte). The largest number that can be represented by a byte is 255 (all 0s are reserved for the network address and all 1s are reserved for the broadcast address; therefore the maximum available is 254). There are three possible types of licence:

- **Class A licences** These were intended for very large organisations and were mainly issued to universities in the US, but are rarely issued now. In a class A licence, the first byte is fixed but the organisation is free to allocate addresses in the other bytes, giving it a maximum of 254 x 254 x 254=16.3 million possible addresses on its network. Class A licences are no longer issued. In a class A licence, the leftmost bit is always zero. The largest number that can be represented is therefore 127 and thus the range is: 1–126. *X. X. X* (127 is reserved for the loopback address – a means of testing the network hardware and software on a computer). Thus, there are 126 class A licences each with 16.3 million addresses.

- **Class B licences** These were also issued to large organisations – many universities in the UK hold a class B licence. With a class B licence, the first two bytes are fixed, giving the organisation a maximum of 254 x 254 = 64,516 possible addresses on its network. Thus 157.228 uniquely identifies the University of Sunderland; the remaining parts of the address identify specific machines. Class B licences are very rarely issued now. The first two bits of a class B licence are always 10. Therefore the effective range is 128–191. *X. X. X.*

- **Class C licences** These are the most common and are still issued. In a class C licence, the first three bytes are fixed, giving the organisation 254 possible addresses on its network. The first three bits if a class C licence are always 110 therefore the effective range is 192–223. *X. X. X.*

Internet service providers (ISPs) either allocate IP addresses statically – that is to say, a machine always has the same IP address (a necessity for a web server), or dynamically – leased for a period (usually 24 hours), after which it needs to be reviewed. Logical addressing is also known as layer-three addressing because it occurs at layer-three of the OSI seven-layer model.

Clearly, few organisations will ever have 16.3 million computers (that a class A licence would allow) and few holding a class B license will ever have 64,516 computers – such allocation of IP addresses has meant huge wastage.

Subnetworks (subnets)

As can be seen from the above, with class A and B licences there would be a huge number of hosts on a network. If we take class A as an example, it is possible there could be 16.3 million computers on a single network. This is akin to having all the cars in the country on one road at the same time – there would be too much traffic and everything would grind to a halt. Just as the road network comprises many roads, the computer network can also be divided into smaller networks or subnetworks (often referred to as subnets). And just as with road networks, such a division reduces the load in each subnetwork enabling traffic to flow more freely. The key to good network design is traffic management (see Chapter 7).

The network is therefore divided using a subnetwork (or subnet) mask. As its name suggests, this is a mask (in the form of 4 bytes) that is applied to the IP number to determine the correct network for the traffic. The subnet mask is local to the organisation only (i.e. it is not transmitted outside the organisation) and is found in a computer's settings. In Windows this can be found in the Network Connections box or by running **ipconfig** (Windows XP and 2000) or **winipcfg** (in Windows 98) (Figure 3.22).

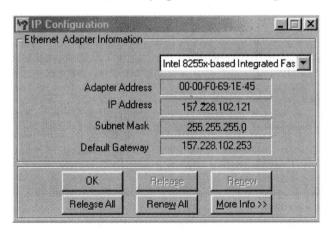

**Figure 3.22: Ethernet settings
(using winipcfg from Windows 98 as it is easier to understand)**

In this example, we can see that the IP address is class B (157 is in the class B range). Where there is a value other than zero in the subnet mask, the corresponding part of the IP address is treated as part of that network. Each part of the IP address is a byte (with a maximum value of 255) – thus in the Figure 3.22 the subnet mask identifies that all the first, second and third bytes of the IP address relate to the network. Thus, host 121 is to be found on subnetwork 102 of major network 157.228 (see Chapter 11 for an example).

Figure 3.23 (overleaf) shows how the **ipconfig** command displays similar information (note that this is a for a different computer than the one show in Figure 3.22).

```
C:\WINDOWS\system32\cmd.exe                              _ □ x

   Host Name . . . . . . . . . . . . : phils-laptop
   Primary Dns Suffix  . . . . . . . :
   Node Type . . . . . . . . . . . . : Hybrid
   IP Routing Enabled. . . . . . . . : No
   WINS Proxy Enabled. . . . . . . . : No
   DNS Suffix Search List. . . . . . : sunderland.ac.uk

Ethernet adapter Local Area Connection:

   Connection-specific DNS Suffix  . : sunderland.ac.uk.
   Description . . . . . . . . . . . : SiS 900 PCI Fast Ethernet Adapter
   Physical Address. . . . . . . . . : 00-40-D0-37-06-6?
   Dhcp Enabled. . . . . . . . . . . : Yes
   Autoconfiguration Enabled . . . . : Yes
   IP Address. . . . . . . . . . . . : 157.228.113.82
   Subnet Mask . . . . . . . . . . . : 255.255.0.0
   Default Gateway . . . . . . . . . : 157.228.253.2
   DHCP Server . . . . . . . . . . . : 157.228.12.1
   DNS Servers . . . . . . . . . . . : 157.228.12.1
                                       157.228.13.65
   Lease Obtained. . . . . . . . . . : 04 July 2005 13:15:04
   Lease Expires . . . . . . . . . . : 19 January 2038 04:14:07

C:\Documents and Settings\cs0pir>
```

Figure 3.23: Ethernet settings (ipconfig in Windows XP)

Section 4: End of chapter assessment

Questions

1. Discuss how data is encoded on to a medium and why a packet structure is used. You should use any necessary diagrams to illustrate your answer.

2. For each popular networking topology, draw a diagram illustrating the topology and highlight any advantages/disadvantages of the topology.

3. Discuss the terms 'logical' and 'physical' addressing. Highlight any differences and give an example of the use of each.

Answers

1. This question tests your knowledge of network basics. The assessor is trying to find out if you understand the fundamentals of computer communications – that we need to encode data as a voltage for transmission, that we use at least two voltages (and why); and that a packet structure is necessary. To answer it, you need to discuss how data is encoded on to the medium and why a packet structure is used. Wherever possible, you should illustrate your answer with diagrams.

2. Topologies are a common question and come in a variety of guises. Once you have learnt the topologies, tackling such a question is fairly easy – all you need to do is to draw a diagram of each of the topologies and to list their advantages and disadvantages. Drawing the diagrams is an essential part of the answer.

3. This particular question is trying to establish whether you know about the addressing mechanisms used in computer networking. The ideal answer to this question would discuss both terms separately, highlight any differences between them and discuss why these differences are necessary. You should illustrate your answer with examples of both addressing mechanisms and, for extra marks, highlight why the Internet could not run with physical addressing mechanisms. Comparing addressing schemes to either the postal service or the telephone network will impress the assessor and will earn you extra marks.

Section 5: Further reading and research

Cisco Networking Academy Program (2004) CCNA 1 and 2 *Companion Guide* (3rd edn) Cisco Press. ISBN: 1 5871315 0 1. Chapters 1, 7 and 8.

Computer Systems Architecture (2002) R M Newman, E Gaura and D Hibbs Lexden Publishing. ISBN 1-903337-07-0.

Chapter 4
Standards

Chapter summary

One of the most important things to understand when studying networking is the standards involved. The main set of standards that has helped networks evolve so quickly is the Open Systems Integration (OSI) seven-layer model. This provides a model for the development of computer communication and is fundamental to the study of networking. Other models exist, however, the two most important being the transmission control protocol/Internet protocol model and the Novell netware model. TCP/IP is of great importance as the Internet is built around this model; the netware model, however, is seen as less important in the networking industry today. This chapter concentrates on the OSI and TCP/IP models. (The benefits of the seven-layer model were discussed in *Chapter 3*.)

Learning outcomes

After studying this chapter you should aim to test your achievement of the following outcomes. You should be able to:

Outcome 1: OSI seven-layer model

Understand the concept of, and each layer of, the OSI seven-layer model. Question 1 at the end of this chapter will test your ability to do this.

Outcome 2: TCP/IP model

Understand the TCP/IP model and each of its layers. Question 2 at the end of this chapter will test your ability to do this.

Outcome 3: Comparison of the models

Understand the differences and similarities between the OSI seven-layer model and the TCP/IP model. Question 3 at the end of this chapter will test your ability to do this.

How will you be assessed on this?

Of all the topics in networking, assessors feel obliged to assess your knowledge of this subject – the study of these models is like the study of the human body to medicine! Assessment usually takes place in an exam or TCT – the subject lends itself well to this. I have written over 50 papers in the last 11 years and all have had at least one question on these models!

TIPS & ADVICE

This chapter is probably the most important in this book, and understanding it is key to the study of networking. You *should study this chapter repeatedly until you understand it*. This study shouldn't be in vain – you are almost guaranteed to be assessed on it. This is even more true of MCSE or CCNA professional qualifications.

Section 1: The OSI seven-layer model

Early computer networking evolved slowly and in a proprietary fashion until those bodies involved in networking came together under the umbrella of the International Standards Organisation (ISO) and developed the open systems interconnection (OSI) model. This model has been responsible for the rapid development of computer networking that has taken place and which continues to take place. Understanding the seven-layer model is an absolute necessity for the continued study of networking and for most professional qualifications.

The OSI seven-layer model

The OSI seven-layer model (sometimes referred to as the ISO seven-layer model) basically divides the complex process of computer communication into smaller, tightly defined parts that aid understanding and network development (the benefits of a layered approach are discussed in *Chapter 3*). Because the process is broken into parts, it provides opportunities for vendors to specialise in particular areas of networking rather than offering a complete service. This is common practice in other areas (for example, as we saw in *Chapter 3*, with portable CD players). The layers of the OSI seven-layer model were given in *Figure 3.21* in the last chapter but are shown here again for convenience in *Figure 4.1*.

Application
Presentation
Session
Transport
Network
Data link
Physical

Figure 4.1: The OSI seven-layer model

TIPS & ADVICE

A phrase might help you remember the order of the layers in the model. My personal favourite, which works from the bottom up is:

Please

Do

Not

Throw

Sausage

Pizza

Away

There is another – 'A Powered-down System Transmits No Data Packets' – which works top down.

The seven-layer model facilitates communication between any two computer systems that support the model even though their underlying architecture, encoding mechanisms (e.g. ASCII, EBCDIC) and method of storage may be totally incompatible. The model therefore allows totally incompatible machines (such as Apple MACs and PCs) to share data, to send email and to browse the web. The model achieves this by converting the data into an abstract data type that can be understood by both machine types and through handling all aspects of communication between the machines.

To take an abstract example. A French businessman wishes to speak to a Greek businesswoman over the phone. Neither can speak the language of the other and so they decide to use interpreters. Unfortunately, they cannot find a French-to-Greek interpreter in either country but can find a French-to-English in France and a Greek-to-English in Greece. By using the abstract language of English they have a basis for communication. They also need to establish the call (through the company telephone operator), to have mechanisms in place to redial should the connection break, to speak courteously, etc. They may also need to handle delays in the telephone network. *Figure 4.2* shows how such a communication structure might look.

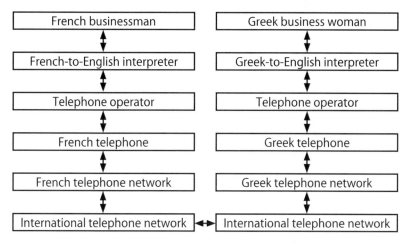

Figure 4.2: Communicating using telephones

As can be appreciated, this process is quite complex: the business people don't need to know how the telephone networks operate or how the telephone operates, the language of the other person or even the number to dial. They simply rely on services provided by the others, but the services must meet standards. The seven-layer model uses the same concept for computer communication, although the functions of each layer are clearly different.

The upper layers

The top three layers of the model are application orientated – that is, they are machine and operating-system specific, converting the data received from the network into a usable form and vice versa.

Layer 7: the application layer

The application layer is the network layer that is closest to the user. It differs from the other layers in that it doesn't provide services to any other OSI layer. It provides the user's application (e.g. browsers, telnet, word processors, spreadsheets) with network services, such as file access, Internet access and shared printing. One of the best ways of remembering the application layer and its function is to think of it as the interface for browsers.

Layer 6: the presentation layer

The presentation layer is responsible for converting between data formats – putting the data to be sent into an abstract form and converting data received into a format suitable for the machine. The presentation layer is also responsible for data compression and is associated with such formats as JPEG, GIF and applications such as Quicktime. The easiest way to remember it is to think of it as the English-to-French translator.

Layer 5: the session layer

The session layer is responsible for establishing, managing and terminating sessions between two communicating hosts. It also provides for the synchronisation of dialogue between the hosts, for session regulation, efficient data transfer, class of service and exception reporting. Effectively, the session layer controls the dial-up box that springs up when we attempt to use the Internet without having a connection. It also controls dialogues and conversations. Think of the session layer as springing-up the dial-up box.

The lower layers

So far we have been discussing information to be sent as data. As discussed in *Chapter 3*, the data, however, must be broken down into packets to be transmitted effectively across the network. It is in the lower layers that the data enters the process of being broken down. Hence, the lower layers of the model are concerned with data transport, whereas the upper three layers are concerned with application issues. This boundary can be thought of as that between application protocols and data-flow protocols.

Layer 4: the transport layer

The transport layer breaks the data from the sending host down into units called segments and reassembles the segments received into data. This layer also provides the session layer with a transport service and shields it from details such as reliability and flow control. To provide a reliable service, transport error detection, error recovery and information flow control are used (think of flow control and reliability for ease of memory).

Layer 3: the network layer

The network layer is a complex layer where logical addressing resides. It is the layer that provides connectivity and path selection between the host systems. The Internet operates at this layer. The devices in it (often represented by the 'cloud' in diagrams) switch the data packets to the appropriate path using the logical address (that is known as routing – *see Chapters 6* and *11*). These hosts can be on geographically separate networks.

The data continues to be broken up. In this layer, the segments are broken into packets suitable for transmission across the Internet. Headers and footers are added to the packets to make them suitable for transmission. The most important elements in the header are the destination address (the network address of the destination machine) and the source address (the network address of the sending machine). Nowadays these addresses are almost always IP addresses – and we can think of them as such (*see Chapter 3* for more information on IP addresses). The most important element in the footer is the CRC (*see Chapter 3*). Note that the size of the data is increasing as we add the headers and footers. (To remember this layer, think of path selection, routing and logical addressing.)

Layer 2: the data link layer

The data link layer provides for the transit of data across a physical link. As it is the physical link, it uses physical addresses. These addresses are particular to the networking technology in use – i.e. we are now becoming network dependent. Whilst the technology itself embraces this layer, it also covers access to the communications medium (*see Chapter 5*).

The data continues to be broken up. The packets are taken from the network layer and are broken into frames suitable for transmission over the implemented network technology. Different network technologies – for example, Ethernet and Token Ring (*see Chapter 5*) – have different frame sizes and composition – just as the envelopes used for letters differ in size between the USA and the UK. Again, headers and footers are added to the data. The headers contain the physical addresses of the source and destination machines, and the footer contains another CRC for the frame. (To remember this layer, think of frames and access control.)

Layer 1: the physical layer

The physical layer is the very bottom of the model and is concerned with the electrical, mechanical, procedural and functional specifications for activating, maintaining and deactivating the physical link between end systems. The data is sent from this layer one bit at a time, perhaps as voltages on a wire. Thus the data needs to be broken up into further bits at this layer of the model. The properties that allow the data to be sent and received accurately (such as voltage levels, timing of voltage changes, physical data rates, etc.) need to be defined here. Maximum transmission distances, physical connectors and other similar attributes are defined in this layer's specification. (The best way to remember this layer is to think of physical properties and bits.)

TIPS & ADVICE

In this discussion of the seven-layer model we have looked at five distinct formats in which the data is converted or encapsulated. From the bottom up these are:

- bits;
- frames;
- packets;
- segments;
- datastream.

Again, a phrase might help you to remember this. My favourite is:

British

Forces

Postal

Service

The data simply comes at the end!

Quick test

List the seven layers of the OSI seven-layer model and briefly describe each. Now amend your answer to show how the data is encapsulated at each later.

TIPS & ADVICE

The seven-layer model will almost certainly crop up as an examination question at some point. The model is so fundamental to networking that an examiner is almost duty-bound to ask it! You may as well, therefore, make life simple and learn it thoroughly now.

Section 2: The TCP/IP model

Although the OSI model is recognised and used universally, the open standard for the Internet is Transmission Control Protocol/Internet Protocol. TCP/IP makes data communication possible between two computers (running appropriate software) anywhere in the world at almost the speed of electricity (consider emails). The US Department of Defense (DoD) design specification for the Internet was for a computer network that allowed military bases to communicate across the world and which was also capable of surviving a war (including a nuclear war). Thus the Internet is a mesh network (*see Chapter 3*) with multiple paths to each location to allow the data packets to get through every time under any conditions. This presented challenges for the designers (remember the Internet was developed in the late 1960s) who went on to develop a four-layer model (*see Figure 4.3*). It is important to bear the original intention of the Internet in mind as we examine this model.

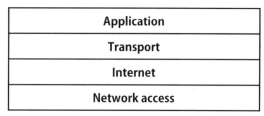

Application
Transport
Internet
Network access

Figure 4.3: The TCP/IP model

TIPS & ADVICE

Just as it is useful to have a mnemonic to help remember the order of the layers of the seven-layer model, so it is useful to have one for the TCP/IP model. I remember the UNIX model as simply:

A TIN

Application layer

The designers of the Internet opted to create a layer that could handle all the higher or application-orientated protocols. Thus the application layer (sometimes referred to as the process layer) handles high-level data protocols, issues of representation, encoding and dialogue control. Just like the seven-layer model, this layer ensures the data is properly packaged for the next layer.

Transport layer

Also known as the host-to-host layer, the transport layer is in the same place in this model as it is in the seven-layer model. As with the seven-layer model, data is segmented within this layer ready for the next layer. The transport layer provides some of the protocols that are used to send data across the Internet. Specifically, it provides the Transmission Control Protocol (TCP), which supports connection-orientated services such as File Transfer Protocol (FTP), Hypertext Transfer Protocol (HTTP), Simple Mail Transfer Protocol (SMTP) and Domain Name Services (DNS) (for domain name lookups). It also provides a connectionless service known as UDP (User Datagram Protocol), which provides a faster but unreliable service. Generally, UDP is used for trivial FTP (TFTP) and sometimes DNS.

Internet layer

This is best thought of as the postal service that delivers the letters (or, in this case, packets) you send. Segments are accepted from the transport layer and converted into packets. It allows these packets to be transmitted from any network on the Internet so they arrive at their destination independent of the path and networks it took to get there. The best route must be selected at this layer (e.g. it mustn't select a link that is down), which is known as **path determination**. The placing of the data on to the link is known as **switching**. **Routers** (*see Chapter 6*) handle these tasks. The Internet layer is roughly equivalent to the network layer of the seven-layer model.

Network access layer

This layer is essentially a combination of the seven-layer model's physical and data link layers. As such it is concerned with all the issues an IP packet requires to cross a physical link from one device to another directly connected device. This is sometimes called the host-to-network layer. Data encapsulation into frames and bits is also handled by this layer.

> **KEY CONCEPT**
>
> Learn the TCP/IP model thoroughly as it is also fundamental to networking and crucial for further studies, such as Cisco or Microsoft professional.

Quick test

List the four layers of the TCP/IP model and briefly describe each one.

Section 3: Comparison of the models

The OSI seven-layer model and the TCP/IP model perform a similar function in that they allow any connected computers to communicate. *Figure 4.4* compares the seven-layer model and the TCP/IP model.

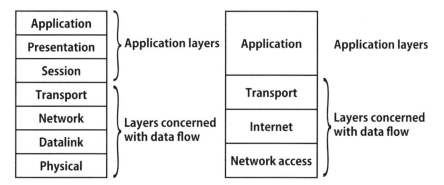

Figure 4.4: Comparison of the OSI seven-layer model and the TCP/IP model

The similarities between the two models can be summarised as follows:

- Both are layered models and, as such, have the benefits of layering (see Chapter 3).
- Both have application layers, although the TCP/IP application layer incorporates the session and presentation layers.
- The transport layer is comparable in each.
- The Internet layer (TCP/IP) and the network layer (OSI) are comparable.

- Both have packet switched technology.
- Networking professionals need to understand both models.

The differences can be summarised as follows:

- TCP/IP appears simpler because it has fewer layers.
- TCP/IP combines the presentation and session layers into the application layer.
- TCP/IP combines the OSI data link and physical layers into one layer, known as the network access layer.
- The OSI seven-layer model is used as a guide around which networks are built.

TCP/IP protocols are the standards around which the Internet was developed. These protocols are in use across the entire Internet, which gives the model great credibility.

TIPS & ADVICE

Take the time to learn these similarities and differences – it will be time well spent!

Quick test

Draw a diagram that compares the OSI seven-layer model with the TCP/IP model. Briefly identify the similarities and differences between the two models.

TIPS & ADVICE

Try to remember the staple diet of a networking professional – cola and sausage pizza! What does cola come in? A tin! And we all know what not to do with sausage pizza – don't throw it away!

Section 4: End of chapter assessment

Questions

1. Identify the layers of the OSI seven-layer model and briefly describe each one.
2. Identify the layers of the TCP/IP model and briefly describe the function of each one.
3. Compare and contrast the OSI seven-layer model and the TCP/IP model.

Answers

1. In this kind of question the examiner is looking for two things:
   - your knowledge of the layers;
   - your understanding of what each layer does.

   Using a phrase (perhaps 'please do not throw sausage pizza away'), you can construct a diagram showing the OSI seven-layer model. For that 'finishing touch', you can show you understand which are application-related layers and which are networking related. You can also impress by stating that the seven-layer model is used as a guide around which networks are built. Next you need to discuss each layer in turn, highlighting the services and functions in each layer. If you can remember some of the standards (e.g. JPEG, GIF, RTF, etc., in the presentation layer), mention them. Remember each layer (apart from application) provides a service to the layer above and utilises the services of the layer below (apart from the physical layer). For really high marks, you could also discuss data encapsulation at layers 1–4 and the fact that it is a data stream at layer 5 (remember 'British Forces Postal Service').

2. Again, the examiner is looking for two things:

    ● your knowledge of the layers;

    ● your understanding of the functions of the layers.

    Again, use a phrase ('A TIN') to help you remember the layers and their sequence. Draw a diagram and, to impress, show the difference between the application-orientated layers and the network-orientated ones. You may further impress by stating that the TCP/IP model, unlike the OSI seven-layer model, is actually implemented – it is the one around which the Internet is built. Next, a discussion of each layer and its functions is required. Remember to include that each layer provides services to the layer above. High marks will be assured by discussing data encapsulation in the model (using the same mnemonic 'British Forces Postal Service').

3. This time the examiner is looking for the differences between the two models. The starting point is to construct a diagram similar to *Figure 4.4*, which compares the two models. It is worth spending some time getting this diagram correct as it will almost completely answer this question! By using the word 'compare', the examiner is asking for the similarities and, by 'contrast', the differences. *Section 3* provides a summarised list of the similarities and differences. Your answer should include these, but in a more discursive way. However, make sure you make them easy to find and mark! Don't forget the major difference is that the OSI model is just that – a model – whereas the Internet is built around the TCP/IP model.

Section 5: Further reading and research

Most comprehensive texts on networking will provide you with further reading on this topic.

Cisco Networking Academy Program (2004) *First Year Companion Guide* (3rd edn) Cisco Press. ISBN: 1 58713 150 1. Chapters 2, 7.

Chapter 5
Popular technologies

Chapter summary

A network has a physical shape (topology – *see Chapter 3*) and an implementation, a set of protocols and hardware (technology). Over the years a number of technologies have been established but, like most industries, the market has largely settled for just a few. This chapter doesn't seek to cover all the technologies but only those worthy of note:

- **Ethernet** – without doubt the most popular LAN technology in the world. Hugely dominant and likely to stay that way.

- **Token Ring** – a worthy alternative to early Ethernet, which is still around, although it is becoming less popular.

- **FDDI** – up until early 2004, FDDI was still the standard for backbone cabling. Since 2004, Gigabit Ethernet has taken over.

- **ATM** – this is important as it harmonises the telephone network with computer networking, providing the highest speed transfer of external data to the organisation. It has also been implemented inside organisations as a LAN backbone.

Learning outcomes

After studying this chapter you should aim to test your achievement of the following outcomes. You should be able to:

Outcome 1: Ethernet networks

Understand the development, variants, method of access, typical uses and hardware components of Ethernet networks. Question 1 at the end of this chapter will test your ability to do this.

Outcome 2: Token Ring networks

Understand the development, variants, method of access, typical uses and hardware components of Token Ring networks. Question 2 at the end of this chapter will test your ability to do this.

Outcome 3: FDDI networks

Understand the operation, typical uses and hardware components of fibre distributed data interface (FDDI) networks. Question 3 at the end of this chapter will test your ability to do this.

Outcome 4: ATM Networks

Understand the operation, typical uses and hardware components of asynchronous transmission mode (ATM) networks. Question 4 at the end of this chapter will test your ability to do this.

How will you be assessed on this?

The technologies covered in this chapter represent the range of technologies in use today. The assessment of your studies is almost guaranteed to include them. Commonly, assessments are in the form of a design (in an assignment) and, as part of a TCT, questions regarding their particular features. You are often asked to describe the method of access of either Ethernet of Token Ring, or to discuss Ethernet and its variants.

Section 1: Ethernet networks (IEEE 802.3)

Ethernet (IEEE 802.3) networks are the most popular networks in the world, and the technology is continuing to develop in response to various organisations' needs. It is widely implemented everywhere and looks like being the LAN of choice for some considerable period of time. As such, it is the network that is given the greatest treatment in this chapter.

Method of access

Initially Ethernet was a bus network (*see Chapter 3*), and its method of access is known as Carrier Sense Multiple Access with Collision Detection (CSMA/CD). The assembled data is broadcast (like a TV programme but occupying the whole frequency) over the media. The steps involved in a transmission can be summarised as follows:

- Listen to network.

- If it is clear, begin transmission of the frame.

- Continue to listen to the network.

- If a collision is heard (two frames colliding with one another), send out a jamming signal.

- If the jamming signal is heard, stop transmitting and wait for a random time period before retrying.

Figure 5.1 shows two Ethernet stations (A and C) that wish to transmit at the same time. Both are listening to the network: there is no transmission and so both begin to transmit. The frames eventually collide and both are lost, requiring retransmission. The time taken from transmission to collision to the end of the random time period is, therefore, wasted time.

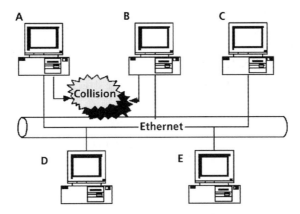

Figure 5.1: An Ethernet collision

The problem with traditional Ethernet (10Base2 and 10Base5) is that, the more frames that are transmitted, the higher is the probability of a collision. And the greater the number of collisions, the more frames that require retransmission. Whilst all this is going on, very little data is getting through, and the users experience severe delays. This tends to happen when the data presented to the network exceeds 7 Mbps. Traditional Ethernet is therefore useful in situations of moderate load and particularly useful for short, bursty traffic loads.

TIPS & ADVICE

'Load' can be affected by the number of computers and the amount of data they transmit.

KEY CONCEPT

It is very important to understand the way the medium is shared, indeed, this is absolutely fundamental when moving on to discuss other networks and other variants of Ethernet. An easy way to remember this is to draw an analogy. Suppose that an army commander needs to get a message through enemy territory during a battle. He writes a note and gives this to the first dispatcher. Both listen and, if all is calm, the dispatcher goes out. Once he's gone the commander listens again. If a shot is heard, the commander knows the message didn't get through and so sends out another dispatcher. The more intense the battle, the more chance there is of a 'collision'. And the more collisions, the longer it takes to get the message through.

Ethernet frame formats

Whatever the variant of Ethernet, they all use the same frame format. As discussed in Chapter 3, data needs to be broken into packets to be sent across the network. Packets are the units used by the Internet protocol (IP) structure (*see Chapter 11*). A particular technology uses a specific frame type. Ethernet frame type is shown in *Figure 5.2*. Being a CSMA/CD method of access, Ethernet requires a minimum frame size in order that errors can be detected properly. If the data to be sent makes the frame smaller than that minimum size, it needs to be 'padded out' (frame contents are discussed in more detail in Chapter 3).

8	6	6	2	0–1500	(46–0)	4
Preamble	Destination address	Source address	Length	Data	Padding	CRC

Figure 5.2: Ethernet frame structure

Ethernet variants

Ethernet is constantly being developed. Early Ethernet utilised a bus or tree topology, whereas later versions used a star topology. The naming convention (shown in *Figure 5.3*) has been adopted for Ethernet.

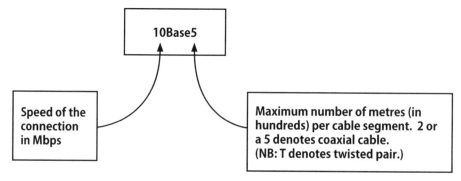

Figure 5.3: Ethernet naming convention

Table 5.1 summarises the variants.

Name	Cable type	Max. dist. /segment (m)	Max. speed (Mbps)	Topology	Max. nodes per segment	Max. segments per LAN
10Base5	10 mm coaxial	500	10	bus/tree	100	5
10Base2	5 mm coaxial	185	10	bus/tree	30	5
10BaseT	twisted pair	100	10	star	2	n/a
100BaseT	twisted pair	100	100	star	2	n/a
1000BaseT (gigabit Ethernet)	twisted pair	100	1000	star	2	n/a
10GE	fibre	up to 40 km on single mode fiber	10,000	star	2	n/a

Table 5.1: Ethernet variants

TIPS & ADVICE

Ethernet is the world's most popular networking technology and, as such, its importance can hardly be overlooked either in an exam or in the real world.

10Base5

This was the original Ethernet development. It is easily distinguished by the thick 10 mm coaxial cable on which it is based, and it operates on the bus/tree topology. Because of the great coverage length achieved for each segment of this cable, after initially being the standard it came to be used as the backbone connecting LANs formed with 10Base2 cabling. Cabling 10Base5 was difficult because of the thickness and rigidity of the cable used. Attaching a computer to this cable required the use of a specialist device, called a **tap** (see Figure 5.4). Figure 5.5 shows how a tap is installed. Other than this, only one networking card per computer (with either in-built transceivers or external transceivers) and terminators were required. 10Base5 was expensive because of the costs associated with the cables and taps. However, current prices are not available as this variant of Ethernet is no longer used.

Figure 5.4: Combined 10Base5 Ethernet tap and transceiver (courtesy of Blackbox Networks)

The advantage of 10Base5 was the long length of cable run, which allowed the network to be extended to cover large buildings.

The disadvantages were the difficulties in laying the cable (due to its rigidity) and the costs of the cable, taps and transceivers.

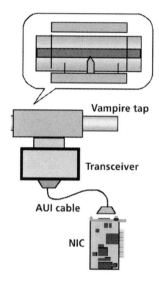

Figure 5.5: Installation of a tap
(courtesy of Surasak Sanguanpong, Kasetsart University, Thailand)

10Base2

This was a very popular variant of Ethernet, mainly due to its very low installation and hardware costs (hence it was also known as 'Cheapernet'). 10Base2 is based on 5 mm coaxial cable (very similar to TV aerial cable) and, in the main British naval connectors (*see Figure 5.6*). Its price made it popular for use in classrooms and for small networking applications (e.g. lawyers' offices, estate agents, small companies and in the home). Adding machines to the network was also easy – all that was required was to disconnect the cable at the required point (when the network wasn't in use) and to connect the new computer. Providing certain standards were observed, the computer would operate. All that was needed to construct a two-station 10Base2 network were two 10Base2 Ethernet cards (NICs) (approximately £10 at the end-of-life price in early 2003), a piece of cable (around £5 at the end-of-life price in 2003) and two terminating resistors (50p at end-of life-price in 2003) (*Figure 5.6* also shows these components). By 2005, UTP Ethernet had taken over and 10Base2 products were extremely difficult to locate.

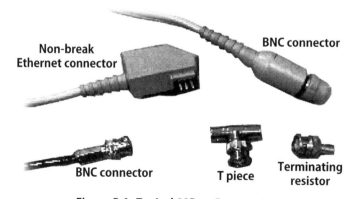

Figure 5.6: Typical 10Base5 connectors

The typical advantages of 10Base2 were:

- its low cost;

- ease of setup;

- the minimum kit requirements;

- the single cabling, which minimises disruption to the installation.

The typical disadvantages were:

- its poor performance for busy networks (e.g. college multimedia lab);

- cable breaks affect all computers (although connectors were later invented to minimise this).

KEY CONCEPT

10Base2 and 10Base5 are both based on differing versions of coaxial cable and represent the 'older' type of Ethernet. Most new installations use twisted pair cabling, as detailed below.

10BaseT

Whilst 10Base2 probably ensured the success of Ethernet as a technology, compared to its competitors it still suffered from cable break problems. Also, in the mid-1990s many organisations were looking to structure their communications and cabling, and Token Ring (its main competitor) was better suited to this. Hence 10BaseT Ethernet was developed.

10BaseT Ethernet is based upon a star technology with a device called a **hub** (*see Figure 5.7*) at the centre. 10BaseT uses RJ-45 connectors and twisted pair cabling (*see Figure 5.8*). This makes the system resilient to cable breaks and also makes it suitable for structured cabling. Thus the management and maintenance of the cabling are somewhat easier than in the past. The method of access is, however, no different. Inside the hub all the ports are connected together just as in a bus topology and so collisions occur and capacity is lost. The network therefore still works as though it were a bus topology.

Figure 5.7: 10BaseT hub

10BaseT is now a largely dead technology with the price of 100BaseT equipment having fallen so much as to be comparable to 10BaseT.

At end-of-life, cabling, hubs and network cards for 10BaseT were priced around £10 for a NIC, a hub less than £20, 100 metre drum of cable £25 and the connectors about £0.05 each. The cabling and the connectors also being suitable for 100BaseT. Thus a two-station network could be set up for about £50 with a hub and £20 with a crossover cable.

10BaseT was popular for large organisations such as universities, colleges, large companies, call centres, etc. It rapidly took over from 10Base2 and as such is being utilised in most organisations as well as in the home. As structured cabling is recommended by EIA and TIA for all new installations; most new installations from the late 1990 used this form of cabling.

Advantages of 10BaseT were:

- structured cabling;

- resilience to cable breaks;

- low cost of components;

- company reorganisation is easier to accommodate.

Disadvantages were:

- capacity is still lost to collisions;

- installation costs are high compared to 10Base2;

- hub represents a single point of failure (as with all star based technologies).

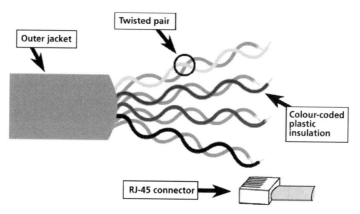

**Figure 5.8: Twisted pair cabling and an RJ-45 connector
(courtesy of Cisco Systems Inc.)**

100BaseT

100BaseT was a major breakthrough in Ethernet technology. Whilst still a star-based topology and whilst still using the same connectors and cabling, the hub used in 10BaseT was replaced with either a 100BaseT hub or a 100BaseT switch. Both provide a possible 100 Mbps throughput, but the hub is still subject to the collisions found with the 10BaseT Ethernet. Through the use of the switch, the ports are no longer connected together internally but, instead, the connections between the ports are 'switched' together as and when necessary for data transfer (*see Figure 5.9*). This means collisions are virtually eliminated as only two devices are switched together at any one time. This allows for a far greater throughput to be realised. Most 100BaseT networks use switches because of their increased throughput – a full duplex switch will allow the connected NICs to realise 100 Mbps data transfer, inbound and outbound simultaneously.

The switches also allow simultaneous 100 Mbps transfers between many pairs of ports, thus increasing substantially the throughput of the network and firmly establishing Ethernet as the network of choice for most organisations. Although 100BaseT still uses the CSMA/CD method of access, collisions are not a problem. Further, 100BaseT is available in full duplex, using two pairs of twisted pair – one for transmit and one for receive. This gives 100 Mbps send and simultaneous 100 Mbps receive.

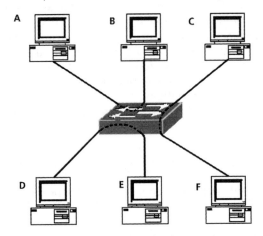

Figure 5.9: Switched ports

The costs of 100BaseT were initially high but, as with most computer products, their acceptance by the market has caused prices to tumble. Switches can be bought from as little as £16 (at 2005 prices) and cards from as little as £8.50 (at 2005 prices) making 100BaseT the entry level network technology. These prices made it possible to build a two-station network for around £32 including a switch and about £21 using crossover cable.

The major advantages of switch-based 100BaseT are:

● the virtual elimination of collisions;

● the high-speed data throughput;

● it was the quickest desktop networking solution;

● its costs are now very low, making it the obvious choice.

The main disadvantage of 100BaseT is the switch, which represents a single point of failure (as with all star-based technologies).

KEY CONCEPT

In 2005, 100BaseT was the EIA/TIA's recommended desktop networking standard.

100BaseFx

In 1995, a version of 100Base Ethernet was devised for backbone applications that ran over fibre. It never really caught on as FDDI was also 100 Mbps, and faster technologies such as ATM took over. 100BaseFx is still available and seems to have found a niche market as a conversion technology to overcome noise problems. For example, if network cabling has to pass through a particularly noisy area such as a motor room, then a signal on a copper wire can be destroyed. By sending the signal as light on a fibre it makes the data immune to noise. It is not a particularly common variant of Ethernet hence its limited discussion.

1000BaseT (or Gigabit Ethernet)

Following the successful development of 100BaseT (which took only 18 months), the Ethernet Alliance rushed to develop the next generation. Unfortunately, this took a lot longer than 18 months, but Gigabit Ethernet was finally launched at the end of the 1990s. Using the existing cabling (category 5) and the same frame format, Gigabit Ethernet is an easy upgrade path for 100BaseT users. Gigabit Ethernet can now be found on servers and in the networking infrastructure that provides connections between switches.

In 2004 there was a major price drop for Gigabit Ethernet; from £105 an Mb in 2003 to £14 in 2005 and a switch costing just £42 in 2005. Again, like 100BaseT, Gigabit Ethernet provides both full and half-duplex operation, offering the possibility of simultaneous 1000 Mbps receive and transmit. Given its dramatic price fall, we may well see Gigabit Ethernet to the desktop in the near future.

The major advantage of 1000BaseT is its very fast connection speeds. Its major disadvantage is the switch, which represents a single point of failure (as with all star-based technologies).

KEY CONCEPT

In 2005 Gigabit Ethernet was the recommended backbone technology.

---

10 Gigabit Ethernet

Almost immediately following the completion of Gigabit Ethernet, 10 Gigabit Ethernet was proposed in February 2000 with Cisco Systems Inc. co-founding the 10 Gigabit Ethernet alliance. The 10 Gigabit Ethernet (10GE) standard was formally ratified by the IEEE in March 2002 under IEEE 802.3ae with the first real 10 Gigabit networking products becoming available in March 2005.

Unlike Gigabit Ethernet (GE), 10GE is a fibre-only product designed to operate as uplinks between wiring closets aiming to support GE to the desktop. 10GE is capable of a transmission distance of 40 km over single mode fibre making it suitable as a MAN and possibly a WAN technology as well as a LAN.

In 2005, 10GE was expensive, costing just over £14,000 for a switch. As this is essentially a backbone technology, PC and server cards aren't really applicable. Initially, 10GE will see deployment in large organisations that require high bandwidth backbones for capacity, backup/disaster recovery or high availability – having such a high-speed link between two sites offers the possibility of remote backup of a server farm. As with GE, prices will fall as the technology becomes more widely adopted.

Wireless LAN (WLAN)

WLANs are an alternative to conventional wired networks. In 2001 many products were developed and 2002 saw their take-up into organisations (in particular hotels and airports). Since 2002, the deployment of wireless LANs has been phenomenal and they are now commonplace just about everywhere – in the office, coffee shops, fast food chains, the home, railway stations, and even in the trains themselves.

WLANs offer a very flexible alternative to current wired networks by utilising radio waves as the medium of transmission rather than copper or fibre cabling (*Figure 5.10*). WLANs operate in much the same way as conventional Ethernet – on a CSMA/CD basis, but provide less bandwidth than conventional wired systems.

Wireless LANs were first proposed in 1991 with the formation of the Wireless Ethernet Compatibility Alliance (WECA) – which later changed its name to WiFi. In June 1997, the IEEE released the 802.11 standard for wireless network. Just as the 802.3 Ethernet standards allow for transmission over multiple media, so does the 802.11 standard. Specified media includes:

- infrared light;
- 2.4 Ghz frequency band;
- 5 Ghz frequency band.

The latter are the preferred choice since they can give omni-directional coverage and suffer less interference (from other light sources) than infrared. The following table summarises the various standards available in 2005.

Standard	Ratified	Network	Frequency	Speed
802.11	1997	Proprietary	2.4 Ghz	1-2 Mbps
802.11a	2000	Standards based	2.4 Ghz	1-2 Mbps, later 11 Mbps
802.11b	2000	Standards based	2.4 Ghz, later 5 Ghz	11 Mbps, later 54 Mbps
802.11g	2002	Standards based	5 Ghz	54 Mbps

It must be remembered that access to WLANs is similar to that of Ethernet based upon hub technology – the bandwidth is shared between all the users of a wireless access point. Thus the 54 Mbps of 802.11g is shared amongst all wireless devices using the access point and performance can be well below that expected – particularly as it is difficult to control the number of users of an access point, unlike a hub, which is limited by the number of ports.

Set up of WLANs is very simple. You need an access point (essentially a radio transceiver) that connects to the network. This connection is usually a UTP connection and commonly supplies power to the transceiver as well as connection to the organisational LAN. Each PC, laptop or PDA connecting to the WLAN needs a WLAN card installed and may need registering as being able to use the WLAN. After that, you are ready to go.

Normal rules governing radio transmission apply, i.e. the closer you are to the access point the stronger the signal and the better the speed of connection. As you move to the fringes of radio coverage, the signal becomes weak and speed is stepped down. Placement of access points is also crucial – see Chapter 7.

In 2005, a typical 54 Mbps wireless access point cost £44 and a typical PCMCIA 54 Mbps wireless access NIC about £24 – comparable with conventional wired LANs but requiring fewer cables to be installed, meaning less disruption to business and lower installation costs.

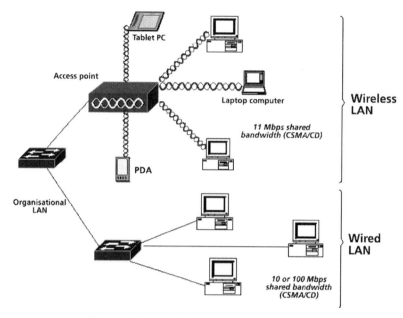

Figure 5.10: Typical WLAN implementation

As well as being deployed to the device, WLANs are becoming a popular technology for extending networks, particularly between buildings. By using a wireless bridge (*see Chapter 7*) and an appropriate antenna, buildings up to 32 km (20 miles) can be connected at speeds of up to 11 Mbps. Deployment of WLANs in such a way is very cost effective for an organisation compared to leasing a data link from a service provider. Even if it is two buildings on a campus, the cost of laying a cable between them is likely to be significantly more expensive than the appropriate wireless LAN kit. *Figure 5.11* shows typical deployment of wireless LAN for inter-building communication.

Figure 5.11: Typical deployment of a wireless LAN for inter-building communication (image courtesy of Cisco Systems Inc.)

Figure 5.12 shows a Cisco Aironet 1400 outdoor WLAN bridge and *Figure 5.13* shows a selection of WLAN antennas.

**Figure 5.12: Cisco Aironet 1400 outdoor WLAN bridge
(image courtesy of Cisco Systems Inc.)**

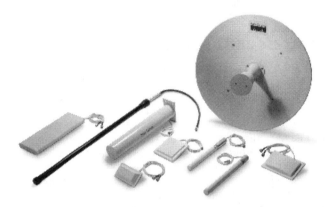

**Figure 5.13: A selection of WLAN antennas
(image courtesy of Cisco Systems Inc.)**

We may well see broadband services being distributed to the home via WLAN technology in the future as the costs of implementation will be dramatically less than installing ground cabling.

The major advantages of WLANs are:

- easy and low cost installation;
- ability to provide connection unobtrusively, e.g. airline lounges;
- rapid deployment;
- mobility.

Disadvantages of WLANs are:

- slow speed;
- security issues (although these are addressed, there is still a fear of eavesdropping);
- increased radio waves in the working environment and associated health worries.

Quick test

Briefly list the main variants of Ethernet, together with their advantages and disadvantages.

Section 2: Token Ring (IEEE 802.5)

Token Ring was developed by IBM and accepted by the International Standards Organisation and the IEEE. It was a popular alternative to Ethernet, particularly with companies who needed a guaranteed response time from their network. Unfortunately, Token Ring never became as cheap as Ethernet and, so, never became as popular. At one point, Token Ring was far faster than Ethernet with its 16 Mbps version (compared with Ethernet's 10 Mbps). Token Ring's method of access is also much fairer, which means it is able to use the whole bandwidth.

Token Ring has been included in this chapter to show there are alternatives to Ethernet, but it is regarded as an end-of-life technology. You may well also meet Token Ring in your employment.

Method of access and operation

As Token Ring is based upon a ring technology (*see Figure 5.14*), the best place to start is with its method of access. A data frame (called the 'free token') circulates continually, passing through each machine on the network. When a machine (e.g. A) wishes to transmit data, it waits for the free token to pass through its interface. When a free token passes its interface, it sets the free token bit to indicate that this frame is now busy. It then inserts its data (including the source and destination address) into the frame. This data frame then circulates around the network until it reaches the destination machine (e.g. C). The destination machine copies the data and sets flags (in the frame) to say that the address was recognised and the data copied. The frame continues to circulate until it reaches the sender. When the sender receives the frame, it checks to see if the address has been recognised and if the data has been copied. If not, the frame continues to circulate. If the flags were set, the sender removes the data and resets the token to indicate that the frame is free once again.

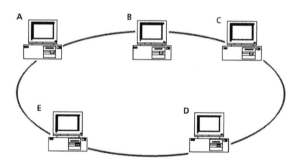

Figure 5.14: Token Ring

However, there are possible problems with this system. For example, what happens if the destination machine either doesn't exist (or goes down), or the sender goes down before the frame is cleared? In the former case, the data packet would circulate several times, but eventually, the sender would give up after several attempts and remove the frame. The latter case is more serious – Token Ring protocols require the sender to remove the data from the frame. If the sender goes down, the data will not be removed and the frame would circulate endlessly. There would be no free token and no other machine could access the network. Enter the monitor station. The monitor station, as its name suggests, monitors the frames sent round the network. When the network starts up, all the machines make a bid to be the monitor station, and protocols determine which machine will be the monitor station and the rest go on standby.

As a frame passes through the monitor station, the station sets the monitor bit in the frame to 1. Should the monitor station detect a frame with its monitor bit already set to 1, it knows the frame has traversed the entire ring once and therefore now seems to be circulating endlessly. The monitor station can then take action to clean up the network by replacing the frame with a free token frame. Supposing machine B is the monitor station, we will re-run the example above. Machine A transmits the data packet to machine C. The frame passes through machine B (the monitor station), which sets the monitor bit. The frame passes through machine C which copies the data. Machine C then sets the address recognised bit and the data copied bit. The frame then passes through machines D and E. Let's assume the sender (machine A) has suffered a failure and has gone down. The switching technology in Token Ring means machine A will be bypassed and so the frame passes to machine B. At this point, the frame is circulating endlessly and so no one else can transmit. The monitor station (machine B) notices that the monitor bit is already set, indicating it has seen the frame before. The monitor station generates a new free token and places it on to the network (in place of the data packet). As a further precaution, the machines 'on standby' to become monitor stations periodically inquire whether they can become the monitor station. Thus, if the monitor station should go down, the network will be able to continue.

TIPS & ADVICE

An analogy to help you remember Token Ring operation is a relay race – you can't run without the baton (the free token) and you must pass it on when you have run round the track once. The baton gives you access to the track (the media).

Token Ring hardware

Although a ring, Token Ring operates as a star format and has, at its centre a Multistation Access Unit or MAU (see Figure 5.15). The MAU simply connects the stations together in a ring but, in the event of a cable being broken or a machine going down, the MAU can bypass the port. Every machine on the network needs a Token Ring networking card. The cable used for a Token Ring is, typically, shielded twisted pair (STP) (see Chapter 3).

**Figure 5.15: Token Ring MAU
(courtesy of Blackbox Networks)**

Token Ring frame structure

Token Ring has two frame formats – a free token frame and a data frame. Figure 5.16 shows the free token and Figure 5.17 the data frame.

Start delimeter (1 byte)	Access control (1 byte)	End delimeter (1 byte)

Figure 5.16: Structure of Token Ring free token

Start delimeter (1 byte)	Access control (1 byte)	Destination address (2–6 bytes)	Source address (2–6 bytes)	Length (2 bytes)	Date (no minimum size)	CRC (4 bytes)	End delimeter	Status flags (address recognised, frame copied, etc.) (1 byte)

Figure 5.17: Structure of Token Ring data frame

Unlike Ethernet, there is no minimum data size for a Token Ring frame. The monitor bits etc., are found in the access control part of the frame (*Figure 5.18*). The operation of Token Ring lies in the detail behind this part. A free token is set to 0 bits but, when claimed, it is set to 1 bit. Similarly, the monitor bit has a value of 1 when set. As *Figure 5.18* suggests, Token Ring allows for priorities to be set. When it is waiting to transmit, if a station receives a busy token it can place its assigned priority number into the reservation field. When the machine currently holding the free token releases it, the reservation field is moved to the priority field. Thus only the bidder (or one with higher priority) is able to claim this 'priority token'. This allows for the support of stations with priority traffic (e.g. real-time data for robot control or applications with synchronous data flows of (low-rate) video).

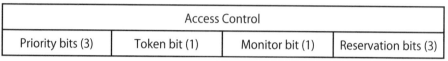

Access Control			
Priority bits (3)	Token bit (1)	Monitor bit (1)	Reservation bits (3)

Figure 5.18: Structure of the access control part of the data frame

Advantages/disadvantages of Token Ring

Token Ring has the following advantages:

- It is a much fairer method of access.
- Bandwidth is not lost to collisions.
- Performance is more predictable (adding an extra machine will slow the network down proportionately).
- Speed (compared with standard 10Base5 and 10Base2 Ethernet).
- Signal quality is greater as each machine regenerates the signal. Token Ring networks, therefore, can span a greater distance.
- It is able to prioritise data flows.

Its disadvantages are as follows:

- Costs are much higher than Ethernet.
- Speed is not as great as 100BaseT.

Quick test
Briefly describe the mode of operation of a Token Ring network.

TIPS & ADVICE

Token Ring and Ethernet are two of the most popular technologies ever. In an exam you are sometimes asked to compare and contrast these technologies.

Section 3: Fibre-Distributed Data Interface (FDDI)

FDDI is also an end-of-life technology, but has been included as you may meet such legacy systems. In 2003, it was still the recommended network backbone – now it is Gigabit Ethernet.

Method of access and operation

FDDI operates in a similar manner to Token Ring and it is also based on a ring topology. It uses fibre optic cabling (*see Figure 5.19*) and offers speeds of up to 100 Mbps in private networks. Its dual concentric rings also provide greater resilience to cable breaks (if one cable is cut or breaks, the data can use the other cable). One of the rings operates in a clockwise fashion and the other anti-clockwise to ensure all nodes are in reach. FDDI uses the same method of operation and access to the media as Token Ring networks and it uses similar flags for recognised address and data copied. FDDI is used in backbone cabling and to link together networking devices, such as switches and hubs (*see Chapter 6*), as shown in *Figure 5.20*.

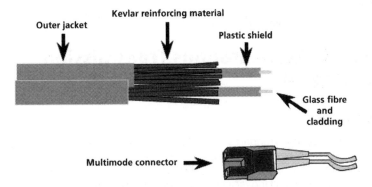

Figure 5.19: Fibre optic cabling (courtesy of Cisco Systems Inc.)

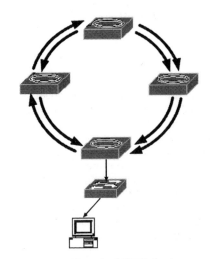

Figure 5.20: A typical FDDI deployment

Advantages/disadvantages of FDDI

The major advantages of FDDI are as follows:

- Its speed as compared with such technologies as conventional Ethernet and Token Ring (FDDI was available when 10Base2 was the standard for LAN cabling).

- Its robustness.

- The distance it can cover – fibre optic can carry data further than copper without the need for signal regeneration (2 km between nodes).

75

- Its resistance to interference (fibre optic is virtually immune to interference from outside sources – *see Chapter 3*).

- Its suitability for interconnecting buildings. (Copper is dangerous as it could be struck by lightning and conduct the current.)

The major disadvantages of FDDI are as follows:

- Its speed when compared to Gigabit Ethernet.

- It is not in harmony with the telephone network and therefore slower over public networks.

Quick test

Briefly describe an FDDI network and its uses.

Section 4: Asynchronous Transmission Method (ATM)

Introduction

The telecommunications standards of the late 1990s were primarily designed to carry voice. This was a time when computers were less powerful and slower than today. The design criteria for these networks specified reliability rather than speed and, hence, the criteria included error-checking facilities. The computing world is now very different, and ATM was devised as part of a review of telecommunications. ATM operates in harmony with the telecommunications network and provides organisations with a high-speed link to the outside world. As it is half as fast again as FDDI, it was also used as a backbone inside organisations.

ATM

As noted, ATM was a breakthrough in communications technology. When used as a network backbone, ATM provides 155 Mbps transfer speed – higher than any available before. However, that was only the beginning. ATM was originally developed for public broadband networks but became the technology of choice for private networks and LANs. ATM is a packet-switching multiplexing transmission technique that makes use of fixed-length packets (called **cells**). Based around switches (called **cellplexes**) like FDDI, the cellplexes identify the cells' destinations and then forward them. This means that ATM responds reasonably well to demands but, and more importantly, it can handle any type of content – cells could also be data, video, audio or speech. Just as network interface cards are a standard part of in the ISO seven-layer model, ATM is a standard in the digital telecommunications protocol. Because of this, it is able to work internally and externally at 155 Mbps. This speed was a major breakthrough: the best external data rate available in the UK jumped from 2 Mbps to 155 Mbps with the introduction of ATM. *Figure 5.21* shows a typical ATM implementation. Many high-end server manufacturers (e.g. Sun Microsystems) manufactured servers with in-built ATM support.

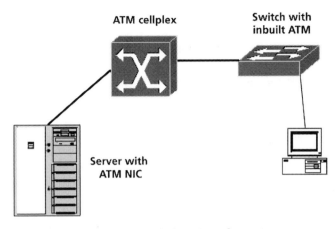

Figure 5.21: A typical ATM configuration

Advantages/disadvantages of ATM

ATM has the following advantages:

- It is harmonised with the telephone network, providing 155 Mbps connection external to the organisation.

- It has a higher speed than FDDI.

The disadvantages of ATM include the following:

- costs (compared with the gigabit Ethernet); and

- speed (compared with the gigabit Ethernet).

KEY CONCEPT

ATM was truly revolutionary, representing the harmonisation of the telephone and data networks. As an international standard, ATM paves the way for high-speed international data links.

Quick test

Briefly describe an ATM network and outline why it is so revolutionary.

Section 5: End of chapter assessment

Questions

1. Discuss the mode of access of Ethernet technology, and outline the major developments of this technology.

2. Discuss the way Token Ring operates. Highlight its advantages and disadvantages compared to conventional (10Base2 and 10Base5) Ethernet.

3. Discuss FDDI technology, highlighting its mode of operation and typical uses.

4. Discuss ATM technology, explaining why ATM is so revolutionary.

Answers

1. This question in one form or another is very popular in assessments and exams. Such is the importance of the technology that the examiner is almost obliged to test you on it! What the examiner is essentially looking for is that you:

   - understand the method of accessing the media (CSMA/CD);

   - understand that it is unfair and can result in a large amount of wasted bandwidth;

   - can sensibly discuss its shortcomings.

   Once you have demonstrated this you should aim to discuss each variant within the technology. For each you should discuss:

   - its topology and typical configuration;

   - the speeds attainable;

   - the distances covered and typical costs;

   - typical connectors and wiring;

   - typical applications;

   - advantages and disadvantages.

   You should then summarise your answer, drawing conclusions relevant to the question.

2. To answer this you need to highlight the way in which Token Ring technology operates and draw out the fact that it is a much fairer method of access than CSMA/CD. You should outline the typical structure of Token Ring, its topology and typical applications. It is important that you highlight that the expected delay for Token Ring is proportional to the number of stations connected. You should next compare and contrast Token Ring with Ethernet and highlight the relevant advantages and disadvantages of each. In doing this you will need to discuss each one with respect to the various stages of Ethernet development.

3. To answer this question you will need to highlight the mode of operation of Token Ring networks and the fact that FDDI is essentially the same. You should outline the topology and typical cabling solutions of the network and ideally show these diagrammatically. You should also outline the speeds attainable by FDDI and its typical applications. It is worth pointing out that fibre covers a longer distance than copper and is less susceptible to noise and errors than copper. Also highlight the fact that FDDI was the EIA/TIA recommended backbone for many years.

4. To answer this you will need to discuss ATM technology. In particular, the assessor is looking for your ability to discuss what is so radical about this technology and the major breakthrough it represents. Don't disappoint – demonstrate you know it is an internationally agreed standard in harmony with the telephone network. You should also mention that it was used by organisations for a number of years as a backbone as it was faster than FDDI technology. However, you should note that take-up was not tremendous as Gigabit technology was on the horizon. You must make sure you mention that ATM is in harmony with the telecommunications network and that it can be provide high-speed links externally to the organisation.

Section 6: Further reading and research

Cisco Networking Academy Program (2004) *CCNC 1 and 2 Companion Guide* (3rd edn). Cisco Press. ISBN: 1 58713 150 1. Chapter 6.

www.bt.com (you can find the prices for external lines from here – e.g. ATM).

Chapter 6
Popular networking devices

Chapter summary

The purpose of a network is to interconnect computers to facilitate the transfer of data. To achieve this, a number of networking devices are available. The principal ones are:

- NICs;
- modem;
- repeater;
- hub;
- bridge;

- switch;
- router;
- Multi Layer Protocol Switch (MPLS)/ Router Switch Module (RSM)
- gateway.

Each is explored in turn in this chapter.

Learning outcomes

After studying this chapter you should aim to test your achievement of the following outcomes. You should be able to:

Outcome 1: Interconnection provided by a network interface card (NIC)
Understand what a NIC is and its essential role in networking.

Outcome 2: Collision and broadcast domains
Understand what is meant by the terms collision and broadcast domain and understand which devices provide containment.

Outcome 3: Interconnection based on a repeater
Understand the function, interconnections and typical uses of a repeater.

Outcome 4: Interconnection based on a hub
Understand the function, interconnections and typical uses of a hub.

Outcome 5: Interconnection based on a bridge
Understand the function, interconnections and typical uses of a bridge.

Outcome 6: Interconnection based on a switch
Understand the function, interconnections and typical uses of a switch.

Outcome 7: Interconnection based on a MAU
Understand the function, interconnections and typical uses of a MAU.

Outcome 8: Interconnection based on a router
Understand the function, interconnections and typical uses of a router.

Outcome 9: Interconnection based upon RSM/MPLS
Understand the function, interconnection and typical uses of an RSM/MPLS.

Outcome 10: Interconnection based around a gateway
Understand the need for a gateway and its role in internetworking.

How will you be assessed on this?

Understanding the function of networking devices is usually assessed in one of two ways: either directly in an examination or TCT question, or indirectly through a design-type assignment. A typical TCT question is given at the end of this chapter.

Section 1: Interconnection provided by a Network Interface Card (NIC)

Introduction

NICs are a crucial part of networking, allowing the computer to be connected to the network.

TIPS & ADVICE

You may recall that, in *Chapter 3*, we compared networking to plumbing. We will again use this analogy as networking interconnecting devices can often be described more easily this way.

An NIC is a printed circuit board that goes inside a host computer (known as a **host**) to provide it with LAN connectivity. NICs fit into a PC's expansion slot (*Figure 6.1* shows three NICs, the oldest being from the 1980s and the smallest from 1998). NICs are also known as **network adaptors**. They are manufactured to operate with a particular networking technology and particular variants of that technology. For example, a 10Base2 networking card is usually different from a 10BaseT networking card because of the difference in the cabling.

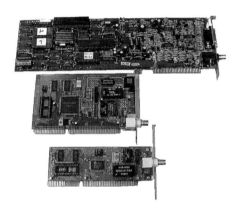

Figure 6.1: Typical network interface cards

In laptop computers, NICs are usually PCMCIA devices. Such is the popularity of Ethernet that most computers come with Ethernet NICs built in.

The NIC's function is to connect the host to the network media, and it is the basic hardware component of network communications. The NIC translates the parallel signals produced by the computer into serial signals suitable for transmission across the network. The binary 1s or 0s are usually turned into electrical pulses or, sometimes, into light or radio waves suitable for transmission over the medium. To make this transmission, the NIC needs a transceiver unit. Most NICs for Ethernet (except 10Base5) have this built in.

NICs are layer two devices in the OSI seven-layer model as they work on frames and have media access control capabilities – including (in the case of Ethernet) an address that is unique in the world. This address is a 48-bit number (usually expressed in hexadecimal). The first 24 bits are a vendor ID and the second 24 a vendor-assigned unique serial number within that ID.

It is important to consider the computer's architecture when selecting an NIC, for two reasons. First, the NIC must match the host computer's architecture (e.g. an ISA will not connect to a PCI-only architecture). Secondly, the architecture should be capable of supporting the NIC's speed requirements (e.g. a 100BaseT ISA network card could never achieve more than 8 Mbps as that is the speed limit of the ISA architecture). Other important factors to consider when selecting an NIC are:

- the operating system (are the NIC drivers supported?);
- the media type (UTP, coaxial);
- the network architecture;
- the data transfer speed.

TIPS & ADVICE

In plumbing terms, the NIC is the equivalent of the water inlet/waste outlet on a washing machine. The water inlet gives the washing machine access to the services of the water network. The drains then provide services for output.

Quick test
Briefly outline the function of an NIC and the factors that should influence their choice.

Section 2: Collision and broadcast domains

Introduction

There are two major considerations when discussing a networking kit based upon Ethernet technology. As we saw in *Chapter 5*, Ethernet method of access (CSMA/CD) causes collisions, which can be a major problem as these waste bandwidth and can cause delays. There is also the possibility of broadcasting a transmission to all the stations on the network. It is essential you appreciate these considerations before looking at networking hardware in more detail.

Broadcast domain

As noted above, it is often necessary to send a message to every machine on a network. System administrators often need to alert all users about a problem, an impending shutdown, etc. Indeed, broadcasts are a normal part of Ethernet operation. To obtain a MAC address of a destination computer, the sender will broadcast asking for the machine with a given IP address to respond with its MAC address (this is known as Address Resolution Protocol (ARP)). To broadcast, the broadcast address (all the 1s in Ethernet) is placed into the destination address field of the frame. Every machine on the network will then receive this frame. If a great many machines send out broadcasts at once, this places an unnecessarily heavy load on the LAN. Ideally, the number of machines that receive this broadcast should be limited or they should be grouped together in some way. Such groupings are termed **broadcast domains**. A networking kit is available to contain such broadcasts – the router (*see later*).

TIPS & ADVICE

Think of a large company with several departments. The sales director may send out a sales update to his or her staff, as might the production manager. However, those people won't send the updates to other departments in the company as this would be unnecessary. They are thus broadcasting the information to their own departments, but departmental structure ensures the information broadcast is contained within the one department – broadcast containment. The departmental structure has split the company into broadcast domains.

Collision domain

As we saw in *Chapter 5*, Ethernet relies on collision detection to operate and, the busier the network, the more collisions. The more collisions, the more capacity is wasted. Thus it is necessary to control the number of collisions to make better use of the available capacity. Given the unrestricted access stations have when transmitting on Ethernet, the only way to control collisions is to limit the number of stations on a network without reducing connectivity. The solution to this problem is to divide the network up to establish collision domains that will contain the collisions. Again, networking kit is available that contains collisions – bridges, switches and routers (*see later*).

TIPS & ADVICE

Imagine there was only one road to serve an entire country. Every car journey made involved using that road. Also imagine there were few regulations governing access to that road – a quick look and on you go! Obviously, there would be a great number of accidents (collisions). One solution would be to provide local roads for local traffic, thus reducing the number of collisions on that main road. Hence collision domains would have been created to prevent unnecessary traffic from entering the main road. Junctions would join the roads providing access but fewer collisions.

The terms 'broadcast' and 'collision domains' will become clearer as we explore each piece of hardware in turn.

Quick test

Briefly discuss what is meant by the terms 'broadcast domain' and 'collision domain'.

Section 3: Interconnection based on a repeater

Introduction

Repeaters are an essential part of Ethernet technology as they provide a means by which the length of a cable run can be extended. As we saw in *Chapter 5*, there are limits to the length of cabling used on Ethernet and these restrictions can often pose problems. Repeaters help to overcome these. There are three types of repeaters – coaxial repeaters, UTP repeaters and repeaters that convert between UTP and coaxial cable.

As an Ethernet signal nears the end of its cable run or gets close to the maximum number of nodes per segment the technology can handle, it becomes weak – timing signals move out and the signal can become distorted. A repeater restores the signal to its original state and passes it on. To do this, the repeater must regenerate rather than amplify the signal (amplification would amplify the distortion and wouldn't address the timing issues). Thus a signal is received on one port of the repeater, is regenerated and then re-timed before being transmitted on the other ports. Repeaters are bidirectional devices that regenerate at the bit level. As such they are layer one networking devices. As they need to listen to a bit before regenerating it, they introduce a delay into the network of at least 1 bit. Repeaters have no effect on collision or broadcast domains.

Co-axial repeaters

As their name suggests, coaxial repeaters are used in 10Base2 and 10Base5 networks but there are strict limits to their use. For example, in a 10Base2 network, all that is allowed between the sender and the receiver are:

- a maximum of five segments (of which two must be free from nodes);

- a maximum of four repeaters;
- a maximum of three active segments;
- two transit segments (free of nodes).

(Alternatively, it is possible to have two active segments and three transit segments.)

A segment ends when 30 nodes or 185 m are reached. At that point the signal is too weak to continue and needs to be repeated. *Figure 6.2* shows a typical 10Base2 layout using a repeater. *Figure 6.3* shows the limit between a sender and a receiver in a 10Base2 network – five segments (two empty) and four repeaters. This rule obviously limits the extent to which the network might grow but can be overcome by good design. By using a segment(s) as a backbone and by using multi-port repeaters, it is possible to design a network with more segments which still conforms to the 5-4-3-2 rule. In *Figure 6.4* there are numerous segments but, between the nodes there are never more than five. For example, between points A and B there are only three segments (including segments A and B).

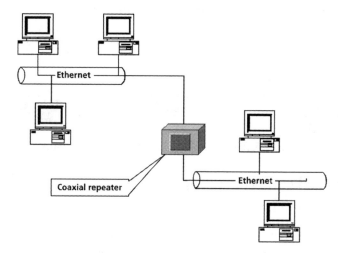

Figure 6.2: Two Ethernet segments connected by repeaters

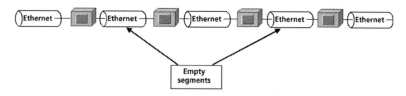

Figure 6.3: A typical 10Base2 network using repeaters

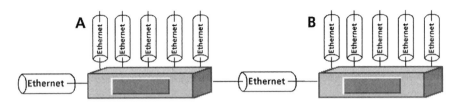

Figure 6.4: A well designed 10Base2 network with many segments which still conforms to the 5-4-3-2 rule

UTP repeaters

UTP has even more restrictions than coaxial cabling:

● It can only have two nodes per segment.

● A segment can only be 100 m long.

These restrictions are a result of the 10BaseT Ethernet being a star topology and because interconnection is carried out in the hub. However, there are occasions when a machine might need to be placed more than 100 m away from the hub. On such occasions a repeater can be used to extend the distance (to a maximum of 100 m either side of the repeater). *Figure 6.5* shows a typical repeater implementation.

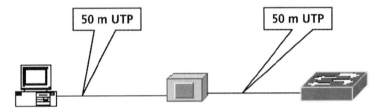

Figure 6.5: A typical UTP network with a repeater

UTP/coaxial converting repeater

As we saw in *Chapter 5*, all Ethernet variants have the same frame format. Occasionally, however, there might be a need to connect machines (or even small LANs) that use coaxial cable to a network based on UTP and, rarely, vice versa. To achieve this, a coaxial-to-UTP repeater is used, as shown in *Figure 6.6*. Coaxial-to-UTP repeaters function in exactly the same way as other types of repeater. Their physical limitations depend on the media to which they are attached. As most installations now use UTP, these devices have become less common.

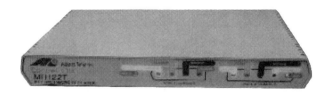

Figure 6.6: UTP-to-coaxial repeater

TIPS & ADVICE

Conversions cannot be made between Token Ring and Ethernet using such devices. Token Ring has a completely different frame structure and method of accessing the network. However, Token Ring cards do function as repeaters in a Token Ring network, thus repeaters aren't necessary.

Quick test
Briefly discuss the role of a repeater in a network.

Section 4: Interconnection based on a hub

Introduction

Hubs are part of Ethernet technology where they connect devices together. Basically, there are three types of hubs: those used to connect coaxial cables, those that connect to UTP cabling and those used to cross media (e.g. UTP to coaxial). Although the media differ, essentially the hubs perform the same function. Hubs are layer-one devices of the OSI seven-layer model. They have little or no intelligence (as standard) and, basically they simply pass the data out across a number of ports. Hubs have no effect on collision or broadcast domains. UTP are the more commonly used hubs.

Coaxial hubs

Coaxial hubs have become almost redundant. They were used to connect multiple bus networks together to form a tree network (*see Chapter 3*). Technically, these hubs were multi-port repeaters. They took a coaxial cable and split it into many branches to form a tree network (with the original as the root) (*Figure 6.7*). As with a standard repeater, the signal out of each port was regenerated.

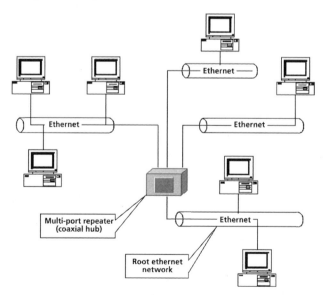

Figure 6.7: Ethernet network with a multi-port repeater

UTP hubs

These are by far the most common, forming the centre of a 10BaseT star network (*see Chapter 3*). The hub transforms the star topology into a logical bus network (*see Figure 6.8*). Whilst this type of Ethernet network is a star topology, because it is 10BaseT it operates as a logical bus. Thus when one machine sends data to another machine, the data is received on a port of the hub and transmitted on all ports of the hub rather than just the port that the receiver is connected to. For this reason UTP hubs are sometimes called multi-port repeaters. As a signal is received, hubs regenerate and re-time the signal before sending it out on all the other ports. This is known as **concentration** and, sometimes, hubs are referred to as **concentrators**. Such regeneration and re-timing are carried out at the bit level, which means that hubs operate at level one of the OSI seven-layer model.

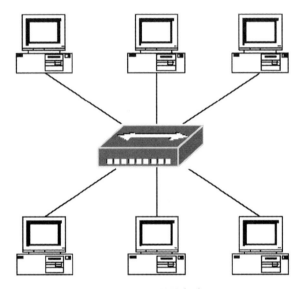

Figure 6.8: UTP hub

Essentially a hub:

- is used as a network concentration point;
- regenerates and re-times signals;
- cannot filter network traffic;
- cannot determine the best path for data;
- propagates signals across the network.

Hubs are most commonly used in 10BaseT networks, but there are some that operate at 100 Mbps. These work in a similar manner to 10BaseT hubs, but simply at a higher speed. To realise the full potential of 100BaseT, organisations should use switches at the centre of the star in 100BaseT networks (*see Section 6 of this chapter*).

KEY CONCEPT

Networking devices are specific to a technology and a topology.

Figure 6.9 shows the typical installation of 24-port 10BaseT hub. In large installations such as this, the hubs are themselves connected together.

Figure 6.9: 10BaseT hub

Quick test

Briefly discuss the role of a hub in networking. Your answer should cover 10BaseT in particular.

Section 5: Interconnection based on a bridge

Introduction

Bridges are an essential piece of networking hardware. They enable traffic control and standards conversion and provide the essential connectivity. As we saw in *Chapter 5*, network technologies are incompatible, but bridges provide the means by which they can be joined. As also noted earlier, the maximum number of segments in Ethernet technology is five. Bridges, however, provide the means of extending such networks. Bridges also provide collision containment (discussed earlier in this chapter). Bridges operate in layer two of the OSI seven-layer model. Being layer-two devices, they work at the data-frame level and are able to understand and forward frames. Bridges can be divided into two categories – those that perform technology conversions and those that work within a specific technology.

Technology conversion bridges

Often, data on a network needs to be available to machines that use different technologies. for example, a production department might use Token Ring technology but the sales department uses Ethernet. Emails and data, however, must be available to the whole company, irrespective of the technology. As bridges are intelligent devices and can see a frame in its entirety, they are able to extract the data from one frame and place it in another. In the above example, the bridge would take an Ethernet frame (from the sales department), extract the data and place it into a Token Ring frame before forwarding it on to the production network. (*see Figure 6.10*).

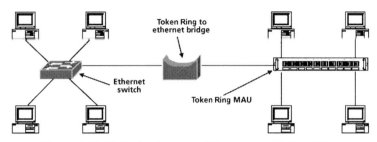

Figure 6.10: Bridging between Ethernet and Token Ring

Single technology bridges

Single technology bridges are the most common. They are used for one of two purposes:

- to extend a technology (e.g. 10Base2) when its maximum length or number of nodes have been reached;

- to perform traffic management by containing collisions and by preventing unnecessary traffic from crossing to the other side of the bridge.

10Base2 was useful in the early days of LANs when, for example, colleges and universities, had one LAN per classroom. When such organisations wanted to join their networks together, the limitations of 10Base2 became a problem (*see Chapter 5*). To extend their networks, a single technology bridge was used that divided the connected networks into distinct LANs.

The most common use of bridges today is, perhaps, for collision containment and traffic management. As bridges are intelligent devices, they can prevent frames passing through unless they are bound for a computer on the other side of the bridge. In *Figure 6.11*, a bridge has been installed in the middle of a busy network. The network designer has made sure the servers and the machines they serve are on the same side of the bridge. This means the bridge will quickly learn the MAC addresses of the connected machines and also which side they are on. Once it learns the addresses it will prevent frames from passing through the bridge unless they are bound for a machine on the other side. All things being equal, the effect will be to split the load on the network evenly – if the load was 6 Mbps before the bridge, it will be 3 Mbps (per segment) after installation of the bridge. The bridge will also half the number of collisions, thus breaking the network into two collision domains.

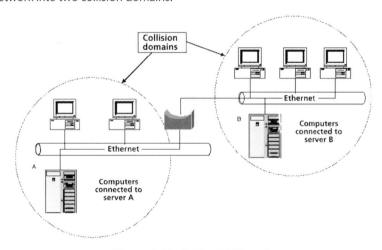

Figure 6.11: Bridged 10Base2

Quick test

Identify the two types of bridge and discuss briefly the situations in which they would be used.

Section 6: Interconnection based on a switch

Introduction

Switches are used at the centre of 100BaseT networks (as hubs were used at the centre of 10BaseT networks). As 100BaseT are currently the recommended standard for new desktop points, their importance cannot be emphasised enough.

Switches/switching

Switches can best be thought of as a combination of a bridge and a hub. As a layer-two device, a switch can read Ethernet frames and can make forwarding decisions according to the MAC address (unlike a hub, which makes no decisions at all). *Figure 6.12* shows the implementation of a switch. If machine A wished to transmit to machine D, in a hub environment the frame would be broadcast out of each port and would be heard by all the machines. The switch, just like a bridge, would know the MAC address of machine D and would know the port it was connected to. The switch would then send the frame on that port only.

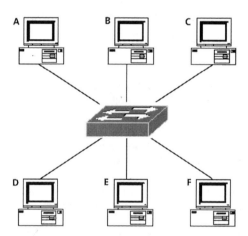

Figure 6.12: Implementation of a switch in a network

The effect of deploying a switch is to make the network more efficient and to increase throughput. Because the data is sent out of the switch on one port only (except for a broadcast), the number of collisions is dramatically reduced increasing available bandwidth. It is also possible for many groups of machines to communicate through the switch simultaneously at the network's full transmission speed. Thus, as *Figure 6.12* shows, it would be possible for machines (A and D), (B and E) and (C and F) to communicate simultaneously, each group at the full bandwidth (*see Figure 6.13*). As the switch only switches the communicating ports together, it is only possible for a collision to occur within a group (in this case pairs) of machines, which greatly reduces the chances of a collision occurring. The switch thus creates multiple collision domains and this function is sometimes referred to as **micro-segmentation**.

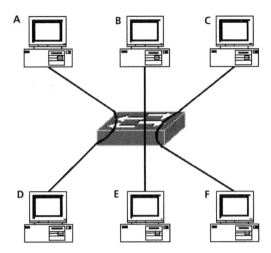

Figure 6.13: Ports being switched together

More expensive switches operate in full duplex mode (*see Chapter 3*), which means they provide each host simultaneously with 100 Mbps transmission and 100 Mbps receive. To use this facility, the NIC must also be full duplex. Most switches are able to accommodate 10BaseT networking cards by switching to a lower speed (known as **asymmetric** switches). Those that are 100BaseT only are known as **symmetric** switches.

Managed/unmanaged switches

There are basically two categories of switches available on the market.

Unmanaged switches are cheap devices suitable for the home or small office. At around £16 (in 2005) these provide the ability to interconnect a number of devices. Such switches do not have the management software necessary for connection onto an organisational LAN.

Managed switches tend to be a lot more expensive, costing around £200 (in 2005). These switches do have management software and are suitable for deployment in an organisational LAN.

One of the key differences between the two devices is the issue of redundancy. Consider *Figure 6.14* where we have a two switch network connecting many PCs. The switches are connected together using a crossover cable (link 1), at this point, either managed or unmanaged switches can be deployed. Supposing we wanted to put another link (link 2) between the two switches in case the first link failed. If we had a managed switch, a protocol called **Spanning Tree** would be running and it would detect the duplicate link and switch it into standby. With an unmanaged switch, no such protocol is running and the network would be brought down via a broadcast storm.

Consider machine A broadcasting an ARP request (sending a frame to all machines) looking for the MAC address of machine C. The frame will pass into switch A, the rule of switching are 'flood out of all ports except the receiving port', switch A applies the rule and forwards out of both link 1 and link 2. Switch B receives the frame (first on link 1) and immediately floods out of all ports including link 2; it then receives the frame on link 2 and floods out of all posts including link 1. Switch 1 receives the frame on link 1 and immediately floods out of all ports including link 2; it then receives the frame on link 2 and floods out of all ports including link 1. The frame is now circulating endlessly – unlike an IP packet, there is no time to live and the frame will simply circulate until one of the links is unplugged. Until this happens the network is unusable as all bandwidth is being consumed by the endlessly circulating frame.

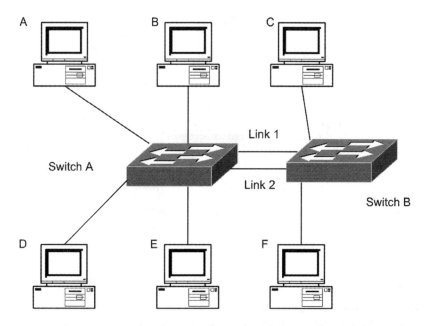

Figure 6.14: Two unmanaged switches connected together

Quick test

Briefly outline the function of a switch and compare it with a hub.

Section 7: Interconnection based on a MAU

Introduction

MAUs form the centre of a Token Ring network and, essentially, have the same function as a switch. Token Ring technology is rarely installed nowadays, and it is often cheaper to replace an entire installation with 100BaseT than it is to replace a MAU. However, there may be a specific reason why Token Ring is required (e.g. it is built in to certain industrial equipment and therefore must be supported), in which case the MAU must be replaced.

MAU

As a MAU is at the centre of Token Ring network it provides the means by which the machines can communicate. Inside the MAU the ports are connected in a ring fashion, and Token Ring frame circulates through the ports. If a machine is active on the port, the frame is passed down to that machine. If there isn't an active machine, the frame bypasses that port. In the event there are more machines than ports on the MAU, multiple MAUs can be connected using the RING IN and RING OUT ports on each. The only real function of a MAU is to make a complete ring from all the active ports. *Figure 6.15* shows a MAU implementation. Whilst the wiring appears as a star, the operation is in fact a ring.

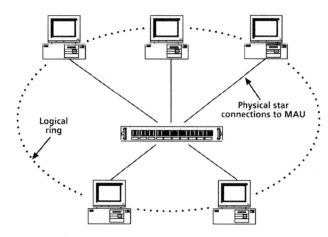

Figure 6.15: Implementation of a MAU

It is the method of accessing the ring in Token Ring network rather than the MAU which ensures that bandwidth isn't wasted (*see Chapter 5*).

Quick test
Briefly identify the function of Token Ring MAU.

Section 8: Interconnection based on a router

Introduction
Routers are perhaps the most important networking device for medium- to large-sized networks. Along with switches, they are the main piece of equipment installed. As access to the Internet is based on routers, it is essential to understand their operation and use. Routers are also the most important traffic-regulating devices on large networks.

Routers
Routing devices operate at layer three of the OSI seven-layer model. Working at this layer, the router can make decisions based on network addresses (or logical addresses – *see Chapter 3*) as opposed to layer two (the MAC address layer). Like a bridge, routers can connect different layer-two technologies, such as FDDI, Ethernet and Token Ring.

The main purpose of a router is to examine the network address (commonly the IP address) of incoming packets, to determine the best path for them through the network (path determination) and to forward them along that path (switching). Because of this capability, routers have become the backbone of the Internet (*see Chapter 11*).

Routers differ from bridges in several respects. A bridge makes forwarding decisions based upon the MAC address and is therefore only useful *within* a network, whereas routers are used for internetwork communication. As an organisation's network becomes larger, it must to be divided up if it is to retain its performance. As we saw earlier, division by a bridge or switch splits the collision domain. What neither of these devices do, however, is restrict the broadcasts. Broadcasts are a very common and a very necessary feature of a network, but need to be contained if bandwidth is not to be compromised – excessive broadcasts lead to what is known as a 'broadcast storm', which consumes large amounts of bandwidth. Because there is no structure to MAC addresses, broadcast containment cannot be achieved by devices operating at layer two (the MAC address layer). Routers operate at the network layer and use the organisation's logical addressing mechanism only for forwarding packets. Hence they contain broadcasts.

Take for example, a typical IP address at the University of Sunderland. Suppose the address 157.228.1XX.XXX represents computers inside the School of Computing and Technology and 157.228.2XX.XXX represents the Business School. The 157.228 part of the address identifies the university and the XXX.XXX.1 the School of Computing and Technology and the XXX.XXX.2 the Business School. In this way a meaningful structure can be given to the network. Broadcast frames not intended for the Business School (or vice versa) will be prevented by the router from being sent to that address because they do not contain the XXX.XXX.2. Hence packets can be routed efficiently. This is the basis upon which the Internet works – 157.228. is the address for the University of Sunderland whereas 198.133.219. is the address for Cisco Systems Inc. (IP addresses are controlled by the Network Info Center (NIC) in the USA and its agents.)

Routers typically are used to join LANs to the backbone of an organisation's network, thus ensuring that the backbone does not become congested with unnecessary traffic. *Figure 6.16* shows such an implementation. Notice how the routers create broadcast domains and how the switches provide collision domains.

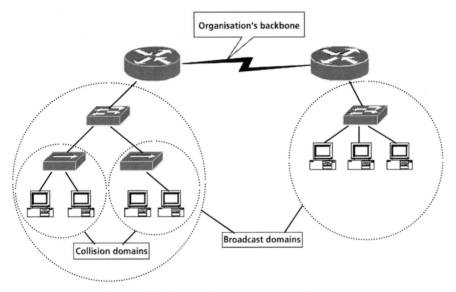

Figure 6.16: Typical implementation of a router

KEY CONCEPT

Routers enable separate LANs within an organisation to be connected. They provide connectivity whilst keeping the LANs separate, and they contain both broadcasts and collisions.

Quick test

Briefly describe the operation of a router and give examples of where they are commonly deployed.

Section 9: Understanding interconnection based around a Router Switch Module (RSM)/ Multiprotocol Layer Switch (MPLS or MLS)/ Layer 4 switching

Introduction

Whilst routers are perhaps the most important networking device, they have one major drawback – their speed. In order to route packets, routers utilise software to determine the next hop and to forward the packet. Software is many times slower than hardware, which can lead to a bottleneck in the throughput. Initially this bottleneck wasn't a problem as the majority of network traffic was kept local. In fact there was an 80/20 design rule which said that 80% of the networked traffic should be kept local. Today, this rule no longer applies principally because of two factors:

- **The Internet** – the PC can now be a tool for accessing and publishing information anywhere in the world with users transparently hopping around the globe

- **Server farms** – many organisations are now hosting their applications and data in one central location with their best staff looking after it. Users from within this location and from branch offices seamlessly access the data as though it were local.

The 80/20 rule has now been turned on its head – only 20% of the networked traffic is local. This has put increasing pressure on the routers, fuelling the development of Multiprotocol Layer Switching (MPLS or MLS).

MPLS

The aim of MPLS is simple – bring hardware speeds to the routing function; but how can this be done? The answer requires thought about the routing of packets – packets usually travel in flows. *Figure 6.17*, shows the flow normally taken by a data packet through two routers.

Figure 6.17: The flow normally taken by a data packet through a router

As can be seen from *Figure 6.17* each packet will flow through the bottom three layers of the OSI 7 layer model in the router. If the device was capable of uniquely identifying each flow, a cache could then be formed meaning that the first packet to pass through the router would identify the outbound interface. Subsequent packets could then access the cache and be immediately switched to the outbound interface. This is known as 'route once, switch many times' and it is how MPLS works. Of course, there is more to a destination address than simply an IP address There is also a port number. MPLS takes into account the port number when building the cache. The dotted line in *Figure 6.18* shows the path the second and subsequent packets would take through a multiprotocol layer switch.

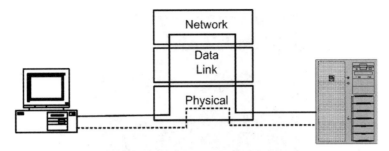

Figure 6.18: Paths taken by a packet through a MPLS 1st (solid line) and 2nd and subsequent (dashed line)

Using an MPLS gives a dramatic performance increase – 2nd and subsequent packets are switched at hardware speed, removing the router bottleneck from the network. The biggest drawback of MPLS is management of the cache and caching the complex flow of traffic. Also, if networks are lost, the entire cache usually needs to be flushed and rebuilt. *Figure 6.19* shows a typical MPLS device – these are enterprise level networking devices with high availability and a price tag to match.

Figure 6.19: Cisco Catalyst 4006 MPLS

CEF

In early 2004, Cisco Systems Inc. introduced another variant of MPLS called Cisco Express Forwarding (CEF). Objectively CEF accomplishes the same as MPLS, but the way in which it accomplishes fast switching of packets is different. Devices incorporating CEF are more proactive and use their built-in router to determine all possible routes through the device, i.e. identify all of the IP addresses on the ports. From this information, a switching table can be built. This table is then coded onto Application Specific Integrated Circuits (ASICs) hardware, which will actually perform the switching. When the first packet arrives, CEF already knows the target port from its switching table and can immediately switch the packet without the need for a router lookup. This further increases the performance of the device.

CEF also dramatically reduces the complexity of the cache associated with MPLS devices and also simply strikes the route from its switching table should a network be lost – the rest of the switching table remaining in tact.

CEF is Cisco proprietary technology and was deployed on all Cisco Router Switch Module (RSM) devices from early 2004. The entry price of a 3550 RSM was dramatically lower than its MPLS counterpart, bringing multi-protocol layer switching within reach of many organisations. *Figure 6.20* shows the 3550 family of RSMs.

**Figure 6.20: Cisco 3550 family of RSMs
(picture courtesy of Cisco Systems Inc.)**

Deployment of MPLS/RSM devices

RSM/MPLS devices are deployed in functionally the same way as a router – in the organisational backbone. *Figure 6.21* shows typical deployment with the devices being integrated with layer 2 switches to service client PCs and servers in the server farms. It is worth noting the redundant connections – each switch is connected to two MPLS/RSM devices for redundancy, load balancing and high availability. The greater number of ports on these devices make this possible at a much lower cost.

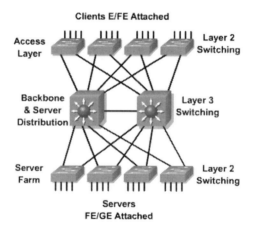

**Figure 6.21: Typical deployment of MPLS/RSM devices
(image courtesy of Cisco Systems Inc.)**

KEY CONCEPT

MPLS/RSM devices are increasingly being used by more organisations as the network traffic flow moves from being predominantly local to being enterprise wide. The internet and growth of server farms are contributing to this new traffic pattern.

Quick test

Briefly describe the operation of an MPLS device and identify why an MPLS may be deployed in place of a conventional router.

Section 10: Interconnection based on a gateway

Introduction

Gateways connect two dissimilar networks together – for example, networks such as IBM's Systems Network Architecture (SNA) and DECnet.

Gateway

A gateway can be used to connect together two networks at any layer at or above the network layer. As there was often a large amount of incompatibility between networks supplied by different vendors, more translation was required than that afforded by standard networking devices. Hence gateways were used to overcome this problem. Because of the amount of translation required, gateways were often slow and more expensive than other interconnecting devices, and they were typically implemented as a software solution on a computer. With developments such as the OSI seven-layer model and schemes such as the US Government Open Systems Integration Project (GOSIP), computer manufacturers have opened up their systems to allow interconnection through standard networking devices, thus negating the need for gateways.

Gateways are, however, re-emerging in small office, home office (SOHO) networking, where they are often used to connect the home/small office network to the Internet (*see Figure 6.22*). In this Figure, machine A is running software to act as a gateway. It has two network connections and is moving traffic between the two networks – the ADSL/ cable connection and the SOHO LAN. Such gateways can be established easily using the Internet Connection Sharing option in Microsoft Windows (98SE onwards). In this mode these gateways usually perform the Network Address Translation (NAT) function – they give multiple SOHO machines access to the Internet through the sharing of one IP address from the Internet Service Provider (ISP).

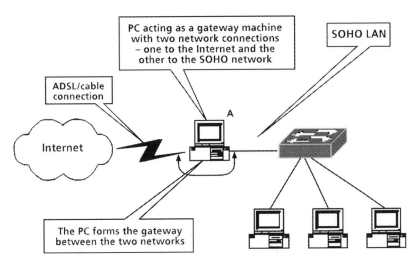

Figure 6.22: SOHO gateway

**Figure 6.33: A typical SOHO router
(image courtesy of Linksys Inc.)**

Quick test
Briefly discuss the purpose of a gateway.

Section 11: End of chapter assessment

This chapter has discussed the major networking devices. Any assessment is likely to ask you either to compare and contrast networking devices or to discuss the operation/ typical application of each device.

Question
Name the eight major networking devices and, for each, identify its function and typical application. If appropriate, discuss its abilities to control broadcasts and collisions.

Answer
The assessor is looking for a simple list of the major networking equipment, which is likely to be worth about one mark per item. The main marks are going to come from your discussion of each of the devices. However, seven marks are going simply for writing the list, so you may as well have them. Once you have completed your list, you can start discussing each of the major pieces of kit. For most of the equipment you will find that a diagram will aid your discussion and also make your answer clearer. Ensure that, when you discuss each piece of kit, you identify the layer of the OSI seven-layer model in which it operates; whether it operates on bits, frames or packets, the technology in which it operates; and, if you want extra marks, what effect it has upon collisions and broadcasts. You then simply need to discuss each piece of kit and identify typical applications. Remember to plan out your answer. If you have an hour you can only really spend six minutes discussing each piece of kit if you are to cover them all within the time. However, it is more likely you will be asked to discuss three from a list within half an hour.

Section 12: Further reading and research

Microsoft Windows Help – look under Internet Connection Sharing or ICS.

Chapter 7
Network design process

Chapter summary

The costs of installing a network are high – not only in terms of equipment and materials, but also in terms of installing the media and the disruption to the organisation. Most organisations are also critically dependent upon their networks, which means they can neither afford for it not to work nor to have further disruptions to repair problems. Network design is the process of analysing an organisation, its current network, its needs and its plans for the future. From this, a networking solution can be produced that will meet the organisation's current and immediate future needs and that can be introduced incrementally. Network design is a specialist process and so this chapter can only provide an overview of what is involved. This should be sufficient for assessment purposes.

Learning outcomes

After studying this chapter you should aim to test your achievement of the following outcomes. You should be able to:

Outcome 1: Network design goals
Understand the five main requirements of network design. Question 1 at the end of this chapter will test you on this.

Outcome 2: Design components
Understand how the positioning of devices and servers can boost network performance. Question 2 at the end of this chapter will test you on this.

Outcome 3: Methodology
Understand and be able to apply a methodology for the analysis of a network. Question 3 at the end of this chapter will test you on this.

Outcome 4: Capacity planning
Understand and be able to apply a methodology for capacity planning within a network. Question 4 at the end of this chapter will test you on this.

Outcome 5: Sample design
Apply the methodologies to a typical scenario. Question 5 at the end of this chapter will test you on this.

Outcome 6: Wireless LAN design
Understand the major considerations of wireless LAN design, the topologies available and be able to design a multiple access point wireless LAN. Question 6 at the end of this chapter will test you on this.

How will you be assessed on this?

Design is normally assessed as an assignment as it does not lend itself to being assessed through an exam. In an assignment, you will often be placed in a group where you will be given a scenario and asked to produce a solution to the problem the scenario poses. This will almost always contain some kind of capacity planning. Design questions in an exam or TCT tend to be limited to a discussion of the process; they rarely include capacity planning. However, if capacity planning is on the syllabus, it may well be tested.

Section 1: Network design goals

In any design process, it is essential to understand the goals of the design before you begin.

Network design goals

Network design is a complex and challenging task. There are many things that must be established and analysed if a network design is to be successful. A network should not be judged simply in terms of its size: a network that contains only a small number of nodes can have stringent design requirements. The goals of network design will vary according to the client organisation and the design contractors. However, the following five criteria are a good starting point.

Functionality

The network must do what it is supposed to do. It must do this reliably and at an appropriate speed. Issues here include performance, reliability and correct functionality. Ultimately, the users of the network must be able to carry out their tasks efficiently and effectively.

Scalability

One thing that is known for certain about today's networks is that they must change to fit tomorrow's requirements. On average, an organisation undergoes a major reorganisation every three years, and the network must be able to adapt to such changes. The network must be able to grow incrementally, i.e. grow without the need for any major changes to the overall design.

Adaptability

Adaptability has two aspects – the network's ability to adapt to changes in the organisation and the network's ability to embrace technological change. Networking is the fastest-growing area of computing and, as such, is continually developing. Any proposed networking solution should do nothing to limit the implementation of new technologies as and when they become available.

Manageability

Networks need to be managed after their implementation. A well designed network should facilitate ease of monitoring and management.

Availability

The network must be available for use with downtime (especially unplanned) minimised. Ideally, a network should be 99.9% available. The only way to achieve this level of reliability is to build in some redundancy to the design, for example having redundant backbone links which will automatically activate should the primary link fail.

Quick test

Briefly discuss the five basic requirements of good network design.

Section 2: Network design components

Designing a network is not just about the cabling and the network devices, but about the positioning of servers and access to the data they hold. As we saw in *Chapter 6*, the different network devices provide a range of services, from network interconnection to collision and broadcast containment. Hence a good design will ensure the network does not suffer from excess collisions, can contain broadcasts and that all nodes will be able to communicate at the planned level of performance.

Network design components

As we have already noted, network performance and network technologies are constantly changing, and so designers need to ensure the LANs they design can accommodate these changes and that performance is maximised by the careful positioning of critical components. When designing for high-speed technologies and multimedia-based applications, network designers need to address the following critical components of LAN design:

● the function and positioning of servers/broadcast control; and

● collision containment/segmentation.

Function and positioning of servers/broadcast control

Servers fall into two distinct classes:

● organisational servers (such as email servers or DNS); and

● workgroup servers (data and applications).

A good designer takes great care over the positioning of servers and of who will access them. *Figure 7.1* shows a well designed network where the workgroup servers (A and B) have been placed close to where they will be used and where the email server has been placed at organisational level. By structuring the network in this way, the machines connected to switch A can use server A without having to use the network backbone (through the organisational-level switch), thus keeping traffic on the backbone to a minimum. If they need access to email, these machines will not cause excess traffic on the machines connected to switch B whilst accessing the organisational server (for email). Access to server B from the machines connected to switch A is possible but should not be used often. This type of design is known as a two-layer network design and is suitable for small enterprises.

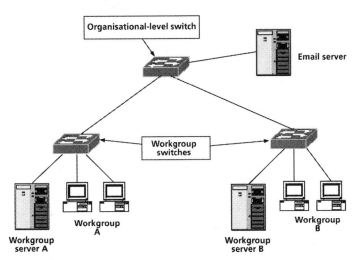

Figure 7.1: The positioning of servers

Notice there is no router in *Figure 7.1*. This could create broadcast-related problems. Because there are no routers, a broadcast by any machine will traverse the whole network, hence wasting bandwidth. The solution would be to replace the organisational-level switch with a router, which would divide the network into two broadcast domains (*Figure 7.2*).

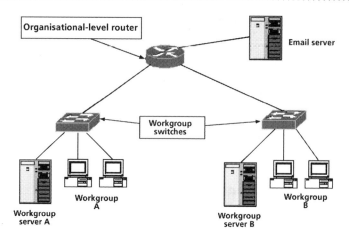

Organisational-level router

Email server

Workgroup switches

Workgroup A

Workgroup B

Workgroup server A

Workgroup server B

Figure 7.2: Router now divides the two networks into two separate broadcast domains

Collision containment/segmentation

As we saw in *Chapter 6*, collisions can be a real problem with Ethernet networks. Indeed, during heavy loads collisions can reduce the available bandwidth to 35%. This is because the nodes contend with one another for access to the network. The designer of an Ethernet network aims to position the equipment in such a way as to reduce access contention and the number of collisions on the network. The single most important device for this purpose is the switch. In *Figure 7.1*, the switch virtually eliminates collisions on each network (A and B) and also on the organisational backbone. Hence *Figure 7.1* shows the correct positioning of switches if they are to reduce collisions. This process is known as segmentation. In a coaxial Ethernet network, bridges provide collision control.

TIPS & ADVICE

Introducing switches into the network segments the network into separate collision domains but does not contain broadcasts.

KEY CONCEPT

The correct positioning of servers is crucial to network design. If the servers are badly placed, traffic may have to traverse the entire network, hence reducing overall performance.

Quick test

Explain why the positioning of servers is of critical importance in network design. Also discuss why designers should consider collision containment and segmentation when designing networks.

Section 3: Network design methodology

Network design is similar, in many ways, to systems analysis and design. The designer needs to:

- gather facts and figures about the organisation and user requirements and expectations;
- analyse the requirements of the network;
- design the structure;
- document the network.

Gathering facts and figures

This process involves finding out as much about the organisation as possible: its size, current status, plans for the building, plans for the future, number of current employees, plans for growth/downsizing, software in use, future software requirements (e.g. changing to a new computer system), management procedures, office procedures, the views of the people who will be using the network, etc.

> **TIPS & ADVICE**
>
> While there are a great many things to find out about an organisation that is considering a new network design, an assessor will want to see that you appreciate the importance of facts and figures – size of data files, number of users or plans to move to a new building, etc.

It should also be established whether data or software are mission critical. It would likewise be necessary to determine what desktop computers are allowed on the network and if there are any protocols that need to be supported. If addresses or names are to be allocated to the machines, it has to be established who in the organisation controls such lists.

Analysing requirements

The information collected must then be analysed. Particular attention should be paid to the requirements of the network over its lifetime – for example, does the organisation plan to expand rapidly in the near future? User requirements should also be analysed carefully to ensure the network will be able to deliver what the users want within the time frame they want it. If this is not possible, the end-users' expectations need to be managed to ensure the delivered network is not a disappointment. Perhaps the most important question to ask here is: how can you tell if a network is successful?

In analysing requirements, the network's availability should be determined. Availability is a measure of the following:

- **Throughput** – how much throughput the organisation expects from the network.
- **Response time** – the time the users expect to wait before the network provides them with the information they require.
- **Access to resources** – what resources the users expect to have access to, and what the organisational policy is on access to resources. This often has to be balanced to provide an effective network.
- **Reliability** – a realistic expectation of the network's reliability (100% reliability can be expensive to achieve!).

Organisations that demand high availability will need to carry the costs of such availability – redundant links, spare equipment, etc. However, the network's required capacity must be planned for (see Section 5 below).

Designing the structure of the network

The network structure relates to:

- the network's topology;
- the network's cabling;
- the connection of devices.

The first two points are, surprisingly, quite straightforward. Current EIA/TIA recommendations state that networks implemented using a star topology should have a minimum of two networking points to every desktop (not all need to be live). EIA/TIA also require that a Wiring Closet (WC) should be placed on each floor to serve no more than 1000 m^2. Where floor size exceeds this, two or more wiring closets should be used. EIA/TIA also specify that a wiring closet should have the following:

- Sufficient heating/cooling to maintain a temperature of 21°C when the equipment is in full operation.

- A minimum of two non-switched dedicated AC outlets (positioned every 1.8 m along the wall at a height of 150 mm above the floor).

- The floor can take the weight of networking equipment.

- Light fixtures should provide 200 lux of brightness and be at least 2.6 m above the ground. The switch should be immediately inside the door. If the light used is fluorescent, it should be clear of the cable runs (because of interference).

- A door 0.9 m wide that opens outwards with a lock to allow anyone inside the room to exit at any time (this may need to be adjusted in the light of local fire regulations).

To determine the best location for the wiring closet, a map of the building should be annotated showing the proposed layout of the computers. Using the above checklist, the potential locations of the wiring closets are marked on the plan. Using a compass, a 50 m circle with the potential closet at its centre is drawn to see if all the computers will fit inside this circle. If not, another location must be chosen or, alternatively, more than one closet may be needed. Even though the maximum cable length in 100BaseT is 100 m, a 50 m radius allows for awkward runs, corner turns, etc. A patch panel lead and a lead to a desktop, will all increase the overall length.

For the main wiring closet (the one that will provide any external connections), it is recommended that the telecomms provider's is used where their cable enters the building (this entry point is known as the Point of Presence (POP)). This wiring closet is known as the Main Distribution Facility (MDF); the others are known as Intermediate Distribution Facilities (IDFs). EIA/TIA also recommend that the cabling is category 5 to the desktop and either fibre or copper between the wiring closets.

'Standard' design structures

As the popularity of networks increases, a standard design structure is emerging based on two or three-layer models. As discussed earlier, a two-layer model is suitable for small organisations. Such networks are effectively divided into two layers (see Figure 7.3). The bottom layer (the access layer) provides access to the network's services. In the access layer are the computers that are to use the network and their servers. These are arranged in groups so that the machines that need the services from workgroup server A are on the same switch as the server. The bulk of the traffic in these groups should never need to leave the workgroup environment. Only email and cross-workgroup traffic needs to pass into the distribution layer. This keeps the distribution layer free from unnecessary traffic, thus helping performance. The distribution layer distributes services to the organisation – in this case, cross-workgroup connectivity and access to email. The distribution layer may well form the backbone of a university/college campus or the backbone of an entire building.

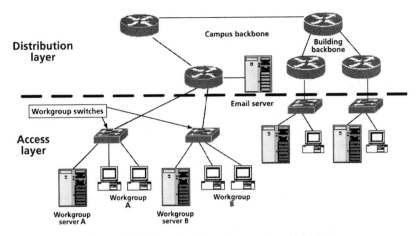

Figure 7.3: Standard two-layer network design

Often an organisation has multiple sites spread over a wide geographical area. In such cases, a further layer is added above the distribution layer. Known as the core layer, this layer provides fast, wide-area connections between geographically remote sites. For example, the University of Sunderland has two main campuses – the St Peter's Campus and the City Campus, about two miles apart. Using a three-layer model, there are distribution layers at both campuses (effectively acting as the campus backbone) and a core layer connecting the two campuses (*see Figure 7.4*).

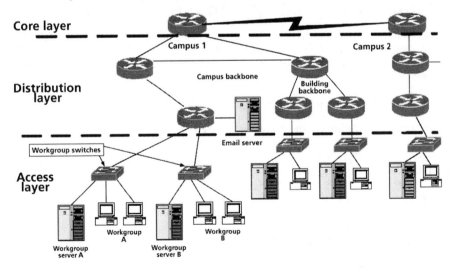

Figure 7.4: A correctly designed three-layer network

Should server farms be established the routers in the three-layer model would be best substituted with MPLS/RSM equipment (*see Chapter 6*) and some redundant links

Documenting the network

The design and implementation stages of the network should be well documented. This documentation will be the starting point should there be a need for troubleshooting. Hence the documentation should provide:

- detailed maps of the wiring closets;
- details of the machines attached to these wiring closets;
- details of the type and quantity of cables used to connect to the IDFs;
- notes about any spare cables and their location;
- details about cabling between IDFs/MDFs.

Troubleshooting is a very stressful task. Therefore, the better the documentation, the faster the network is likely to be brought back up. Documentation should as be full as possible. Also, bearing in mind that 80% of networking problems are caused by layer one (cables, connectors, etc.), the leads need to be documented very carefully.

KEY CONCEPT

To be effective, a network must be well designed. An essential step in this process is to gather and analyse information. An organisation's network is likely to be mission critical and so any faults must be repaired immediately. Correcting faults and upgrading the network are far easier if there is sufficient, up-to-date documentation.

Quick test

Briefly outline the network design methodology.

Section 4: Capacity planning

Capacity planning ensures there will be sufficient capacity in the new network for it to be able to cope with the demands placed upon it. Measuring the capacity of the current network can help to identify performance issues and can also guide the design process.

TIPS & ADVICE

Most questions designed to test your knowledge of capacity planning will start with a set of numbers, that, when used in a capacity plan, produce a problem. The assessors are testing your ability to spot this problem. They write an assignment and deliberately hide figures in the text – a good designer is always on the lookout for hidden information! You should read the assignment thoroughly and highlight every number mentioned.

The capacity planning process

Capacity planning has two purposes: to measure the load on the current network and to estimate the load that might be imposed on the proposed network. Sophisticated tools are available to help with this process, but it is more likely you will be required to measure these loads mathematically. The maths involved in capacity planning is relatively straightforward. It is used to determine:

- the current load on the network;
- the proposed/additional load on the network;

- if there is enough capacity in the network to cope;

- if there are likely to be any peak-time problems (i.e. when the traffic is at its highest, will the network be able to cope?).

To do this, as much numerical information as possible is collected:

- How many computers are connected/to be connected?

- What packages do they use?

- Are the packages held centrally or locally?

- How often are they downloaded?

- What is their size?

- What sort of data is downloaded?

- How often?

- What is its size?

- How often do the users print out from the network?

- What kind of printer do they use? (Postscript printers put a huge load on a network and should be avoided.)

- What are the file sizes?

- Does a file go directly to a printer or to a computer and then to a printer (in which case it is on the network twice)?

- What about email/Internet traffic?

- How often are they used?

- What are they used for?

This should provide enough information about the amount of traffic moved by the network.

However, unless sophisticated software is used to carry out these measurements, the figures obtained will be an educated guess. Allowances should be made for the frame/packet headers, which will be added to the data as it passes down the layers of the seven-layer model (*see Chapter 4*). It will be necessary to talk to suppliers about any proposed applications and, possibly, obtain copies of the software to evaluate the load before purchase. The equipment connected to the network and its operation should be checked in case it imposes a load on the network.

TIPS & ADVICE

File sizes are measured in bytes and network traffic is measured in bits. Remember to multiply bytes by 8 to get bits. Thus a 1MB file is 8Mb.

As much information as possible about the organisation itself must also be collected:

- How long does the organisation use its network each day (if it is open 9 – 5 then it's 8 hours)?

- What does it use its network for?

- Do the users work flexi-time or do they all have the same start and finish time?

- Are there any problems with the current network?

- If so, what weeks/days/times do these problems occur?

- Is there any other pattern to them?
- What time is lunch?
- Does everyone leave together for lunch?
- What is the pattern of the working day (is it like a school/college/university where activities change on an hourly basis)?
- Are backups of the network servers taken at night? Is this across the network?

This should provide enough information about the time period over which the traffic needs to be shipped.

Finally, the design parameters must be established:

- What is the anticipated lifespan of the network?
- Will there be any anticipated growth/decline in the organisation's activities during the network's lifespan?
- Does the building itself contain any physical constraints (e.g. solid floor or ceilings, lots of electric motors, etc. that will cause interference)?
- Should the network be a LAN only or a WAN/LAN?
- Is any existing network equipment to be retained?
- What finance is available?
- What integration is required with other systems/networks/hardware?

Quality of service (QoS) also needs to be determined. QoS basically means the design parameters we noted in *Section 3* – the responses users expect, the network's reliability, security issues, etc.

This process should provide enough information to begin the capacity planning. Remember, answers are needed to two questions:

- Can the network cope at present?
- Will it be able to cope with the proposed changes?

For each question, it must be determined whether the network can cope with:

- the daily load (normally the answer to this is 'yes');
- peak-time load problems (usually more tricky to answer).

Peak times are when the network is under the most strain – for example, when a class begins at college at least one class will log into the network and download software and data to begin their work. Obviously, the students and instructors wish to begin as soon as possible, but the network is probably under its heaviest load during that period – a peak-time problem. (*Section 5* gives an example capacity plan for a college and discusses the issues raised in this.)

KEY CONCEPT

Capacity plans are only as good as the information gathered. Time should be spent collecting and analysing carefully all the relevant data.

Quick test
Briefly outline the stages involved in capacity planning.

Section 5: Sample design

Introduction

In this section we will consider Irving's College of Technology (ICT) to analyse the current problems it is having with its network. We will discuss these problems and propose some solutions. ICT has an IT suite but is having problems with the performance of the network in this suite. What follows is an excerpt from a real assignment I used a couple of years ago.

The 50 computers in the IT suite are networked with two Novell servers using two segments of 10Base2 Ethernet separated by a repeater. The QoS the college required was for the machines to be operational within five minutes of the class starting. Primarily, the machines run a package known as Trainoffice. Trainoffice offers a simulated office environment. In terms of network load, each machine loads the software (30 MB); uses 20 MB of data and, on average, each user prints 10 MB per session. Data is loaded from two Novell servers (old 486 machines). Unfortunately, such are the problems with this suite that it has been closed temporarily. The Principal of ICT is very disappointed about this as the machines in the suite are the most modern of all the college's computers. It can be assumed that classes in the IT suite change every hour.

Process

Although the above is only a paragraph, it contains lots of information. The first thing to note is that the IT suite has been temporarily closed because of the problems (not a good sign!) and that the classes change every hour. Thus the capacity planning involves 60 minute intervals – everything needs to be loaded, printed, saved, etc., in that time frame.

Next we need to consider the figures:

- 50 computers;

- 30 MB of software;

- 20 MB of data;

- 10 MB printed (through a Novell server; therefore 10 MB to the server followed by 10 MB to the printer – twice the load!);

- 10 Mbps is the theoretical maximum from 10Base2 (7 Mbps actual);

- QoS of five minutes;

- 486 architecture in the servers, which means they can only ship 8 Mbps to the networking card (no PCI architecture);

- software and data have to be loaded before startup.

So 50 computers x (30 MB software + 20 MB data) = 2500 MB which, times 8, = 20,000 Mb of data to be loaded before startup. We will add 10% to this to allow for packet overheads (headers, CRCs, etc.). Thus the total is now 22,000 Mb. Before getting into difficulty, 10Base2 can handle 7 Mbps; after that point it is unpredictable. 22,000 Mb/7 Mbps = 3142 seconds. Thus, assuming the network can handle steadily 7 Mbps it will take 3142 seconds or (53 minutes) for all the machines in the IT suite to be ready to start a 60-minute class! Then they will need to save their data and, possibly, print.

There are two possibilities to overcome these problems:

- Break up the current network with bridges and additional servers to make smaller networks that will perform better.

- Install a brand-new network based on a faster technology that will also have better future proofing.

Excluding the cabling costs, the second option is likely to be cheaper than the first and also more satisfactory. My preference would be for the second option.

We need to examine the load under 100BaseT: 22,000 Mb/100 Mbps = 220 seconds/60 = 3.66 minutes. Thus, with a 100BaseT network, the suite would be operational within about 4 minutes (subject to the server being able to handle the load). Deploying this network would require a different topology, new servers (the old cannot make use of 100 Mbps cards), new cards in the PCs and switching equipment. Switches usually come in 24 or 48 port and so we would require at least two switches. If we installed the two-tier architecture we looked at in *Section 2*, we would need three 24-port switches and a further switch to join the three switches. The scenario mentions servers, and the best solution would be to incorporate three workgroup servers (as shown in *Figure 7.5*), each attached to a switch, along with 17 machines (even though this would mean, in effect, only 16 machines!). The new loading would be: 17 machines x 50 MB=850 MB + 10% = 935 MB x 8 =7480 Mb / 100 Mbps = 75 seconds for the machines to become operational. This includes no margin for error but, assuming 100% was left for contingency, this is still only 150 seconds, half the QoS of 5 minutes.

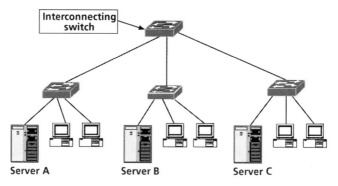

Figure 7.5: Proposed design for ICT

Printing and saving must also be accommodated – this will usually be distributed in the lesson, but may also come near the end; if it does, then it is a peak time problem. Assume that 20 MB needs to be saved: 17 machines x 20 MB = 340 MB + 10% = 374 MB x 8 = 2992 Mb/100 = 30 seconds. The printing needs to traverse the network to the server and then from the server to the printer (it may be on the network twice so allowances must be made for this or it needs to be investigated more fully). This is ambiguous, so assume the worst-case scenario that it is on the network twice: 17 x (2 x 20 MB) = 680 MB + 10% = 748 MB x 8 = 5984 Mb/100 = 59.84 seconds. Thus the proposed network will handle the load imposed adequately. Had this been an organisation that did not change its activities every the hour, this could have been taken across the working day (8 hours?), but peak times should still be noted – arriving in the morning, lunchtime and printing late in the day.

Average load

In this scenario, everything needs to be completed within a one-hour period. To calculate the average load (which is rarely a problem) we divide the total data by the time period. In the 100BaseT final design we have: 17 machines x (30 MB applications + 20 MB load + 20 MB save + (2 x 10 MB print)) = 1530 MB; 1530 MB x 8 = 12,240 Mb. There are 60 minutes x 60 seconds in an hour = 3600. 12,240 Mb period load/3600 seconds in a period = 3.4 Mbps average load. This is well within the capacity of our network.

> ### KEY CONCEPT
>
> Remember, the time taken to get all the computers operational can be calculated approximately by the following formula:
>
> $$\frac{\text{Total data and or software to be downloaded before work can begin (in megabits)}}{\text{Maximum throughput of the technology}}$$
>
> Remember to use megabits and to add 10% to the load to allow for packet headers, etc.
>
> The average load on the network per day/session can be calculated approximately by the following formula:
>
> $$\frac{\text{Total data/software/printing of entire day session}}{\text{No. of seconds in day/session}}$$

Quick test

Carefully work though the figures without looking at the calculations given here. Do you get the same answer? If not, where did you go wrong?

Section 6: Wireless LAN design

All but the simplest, one access point wireless LANs need to be designed. Indeed, even a one access point wireless LAN will benefit from some thought on the placement of the access point.

Wireless LAN design considerations

Wireless LANs utilise radio waves as their transmission medium and so the rules governing propagation of radio waves apply to wireless LANs. It is important to undertake a site survey as part of the design process to gather as much information about the building as you can. There are six main factors to consider when undertaking the site survey:

1. **Data rate required** – the data rate is directly related to the coverage of the wireless LAN, the better the coverage the higher the data rate. Rather than reduce reliability as the signal weakens between the access point and the client (either as a result of distance or signal degrading because of obstructions), access points shift to a lower data rate, therefore preserving the reliability. *Figure 7.6* shows the range and typical data rates available in an unobstructed wireless LAN environment.

2. **Antenna type** – some access points, particularly those designed for non-domestic use, offer a range of antennae. Proper antenna selection and placement is a critical factor in coverage. As a rule of thumb, the range increases with antenna height and gain.

3. **Physical environments** – an access point in an open environment will have a better coverage than a closed or relatively closed environment.

4. **Obstructions** – any obstructions between the access point and the client can affect performance.

5. **Building materials** – the type of building material used also influences range: drywalls allow radio waves to penetrate better than metal or brick walls.

6. **Line of sight** – maintaining a clear line of sight between the client and the access point will significantly increase performance. If you are using the wireless link as a bridge, this is a must as you require maximum throughput.

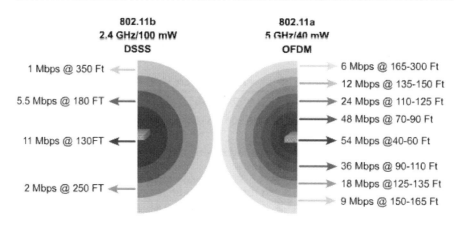

Figure 7.6: Data rates available in an unobstructed wireless LAN implementation (image courtesy of Cisco Systems Inc.)

TIPS & ADVICE

Remember that throughput is theoretical and you won't actually achieve the full throughput. Realistically, for an 11 Mbps 802.11b network you will achieve 7Mbps – roughly comparable to a 10BaseT or 10Base2 wired LAN.

KEY CONCEPT

Don't assume that all wireless clients will be laptops and PDAs; wireless LAN NICs are available for desktop PCs and installation of a wireless network can realise significant savings over its wired counterpart – particularly if the environment frequently changes, for example desks being moved.

The term, device, is used for wireless LANs as often there are multiple types of client such as a PC, a laptop, PDA and specialist products such as supermarket scanners, IP telephones, data projectors, and even printers.

Topologies

Just as wired networks have a topology so do wireless LANs however, the term used in wireless LANs is the Basic Service Area (BSA) which is comprised of one or more microcells – the area of coverage of an access point.

A wireless LAN with one access point is relatively straightforward – place the access point and/or its antenna in the centre of the area you wish to cover. For example if you were placing an access point in a single floor coffee shop then place it in the ceiling in the centre of the customer seating area.

A wireless LAN with more than one access point requires more consideration. The first question to answer is why you need more than one access point. There are three possible reasons (*Figure 7.7*):

1. Provide a coverage area greater than can be provided by one access point

2. To provide redundancy or load balancing in a single area

3. To extend a network either wireless or wired by the use of wireless bridges

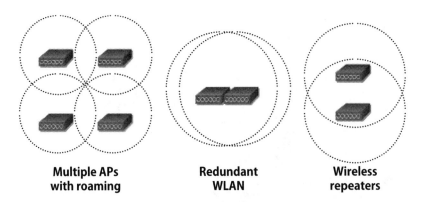

Multiple APs
with roaming

Redundant
WLAN

Wireless
repeaters

Figure 7.7: The 3 wireless LAN topologies
(image courtesy of Cisco Systems Inc.)

Designing a multiple access point wireless LAN

In any multiple access point installation the goal is to have the coverage areas overlap so that a client can roam without interruption. However, too much or too little overlap can cause disruption of the wireless connection to the client. Obviously, too little overlap will mean the client loses coverage roaming between access points, where too much overlap will result in the access points interfering with each other. For this reason, deployment needs to be controlled – consider radio stations, there are never two radio stations operating on the same frequency in the same geographic area, however (in the case of national radio stations), their coverage overlaps so that you can enjoy uninterrupted coverage as you travel. The concept is similar for wireless LANs.

The 802.11b (USA) standard specifies 11 channels (*Figure 7.8*). Thus in the case of redundant WLAN implementations, the maximum number of access points that can be used concurrently is three using channels 1, 6 and 11, which do not overlap with each other. If the density of users still presents an issue then a solution is to install access points operating in another frequency range (e.g. in the 5 GHz band).

KEY CONCEPT

Remember there is no easy way to control the number of users using an access point – as a client approaches if the access point has an available address (of which there is usually 2,048) the device can connect. Redundant WLANs could well be necessary to provide bandwidth – control the connections by getting half of the users to connect to access point 1 and the other half with access point 2 (this is achieved in Windows' device configuration).

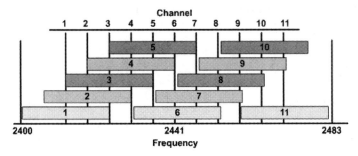

Figure 7.8: 802.11b (USA) channel mapping
(image courtesy of Cisco Systems Inc.)

For roaming solutions, the access points need to be placed so that coverage is uninterrupted and so that channels do not overlap. *Figure 7.9* shows multiple microcells around access points with non interrupting channels.

Figure 7.9: 802.11b (USA) placement of non interrupting microcells (image courtesy of Cisco Systems Inc.)

Changing the channel allocation is relatively straightforward and usually accomplished by browser connection to the access point. *Figure 7.10* shows changing the channel of a Linksys WRT54GS combined cable router access point.

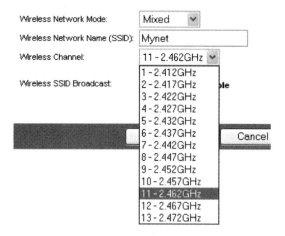

Figure 7.10: Selecting a channel for the access point on a UK Linksys WRT54GS

KEY CONCEPT

You need to ensure good coverage without channel interference – use the above information to provide you with a guide to deploying wireless networks.

Security

Security is a major issue with wireless LANs and can be categorised into:

- security of information in transit; and
- misuse of the access point itself.

Security of information in transit

In general, most concern is about the security of information in transit, any plain text sent over the wireless LAN can possibly be eavesdropped. The question is whether you mind that information being eavesdropped. Most information of a confidential nature will be sent using a secure server and some form of encryption. For example, sitting in a public access area, such as a coffee shop, using a wireless LAN to make a purchase with a reputable on-line retailer. At some point, the retailer will transfer you to a secure server and an encrypted data channel will exist between you and your on-line supplier. This encryption is instigated inside your PC in the OSI 7 layer model. Thus the credit card information being transmitted between you and retailer is secure and eavesdropping the information on a wireless LAN will yield no useful information. In fact, you are probably far more likely to have the credit card information copied down by those sitting around you!

As for the plain text you send during a session in a public access area (which will most probably include emails and any user IDs and password you have for non-secure servers), there is very little that can be done and you should seriously consider whether or not to use the public access area.

If you are in an organisation or your home and have the ability to manage your wireless access point, then there are security options available to you:

WEP – Wired Equivalence Protocol originally used a 40 bit pre-shared key that must match on both the client's and access point (must be manually configured). Most vendors have now expanded this to 128 bit key. WEP protects authorised users from casual eavesdropping and is based upon Rivest Cipher 4 (RC4). WEP is recognised as having security weaknesses; however, it is widely supported.

WPA – WiFi Protected Access. The longer-term security measure is the 802.11i standard but WPA was introduced to address the weaknesses of WEP. WPA also works on a pre-shared key arrangement and although supported by most modern access points doesn't have wide support on wireless NICs (especially early ones).

Security is usually configured via browser access to the access point.

> **TIPS & ADVICE**
>
> A VPN tunnel will provide a secure method of accessing your organisation on an unsecured wireless LAN (*see Chapter 1*).

Misuse of the access point

Installation of an access point without any security can lead to misuse of the access point by unintended users. There have been numerous reported instances of this – one of the better ones is the tale of a security engineer who found a neighbour in his apartment block with an unsecured wireless network. Being helpful, the security engineer used his neighbour's printer to print a document on securing a wireless LAN!

Because there is no physical connection to an access point, it is more difficult to monitor who is connected. Remember, it is not just your bandwidth being 'stolen' that could be a problem – any material downloaded using your access point will be logged with the MAC address and or IP address of that access point. You may be liable for any charges or prosecutions arising as a result of failing to secure your access point.

Most wireless points provide a method of regulating the users:

- MAC Address locking;
- WEP/WPA keys.

MAC address locking

All Wireless NICs have a MAC address and access points will usually have a security setting, which allows you to restrict access to only authorised MAC addresses and therefore NICs. Usually there is a utility that allows you to see all of the currently connected NICs, allowing you to select the ones that should be given access. Obviously, the control is on the NIC – if the NIC is placed in another machine, then an unauthorised machine could have access to the network. Not all NICs support MAC address locking.

When setting up WEP or WPA encryption, the key needs to be entered on both the access point and on the device. Devices without the key can't access the network. As the key is entered on the device itself, the device is authorised for wireless access rather than the NIC.

TIPS & ADVICE

Always secure a wireless LAN, preferably by both MAC address locking and WEP/WPA.

Building-to-building WLANs

Creating wireless LANs between buildings can be a challenging task and is often governed by local planning regulations; there may also be obstacles in the line of sight between the buildings that will impair performance. Clearing these obstacles will probably require a tower for the antenna, which will itself be subject to local planning regulations.

If you are intending to use a wireless LAN for building-to-building communications it is advisable to contact the local planning authorities and seek specialist help at the design stage.

In general, building-to-building WLANs need specialist bridging devices and antennas – see Chapter 5.

SAFETY TIPS

- Never touch or move any antenna whilst the unit is transmitting or receiving.
- Never touch, hold or locate any antenna in such a way as it is close to or touching an exposed area of skin – especially the face and eyes.
- Don't use any equipment without the antenna attached.
- Ensure the environment you are considering is suitable for wireless LANs and the type of wireless LAN you are deploying, e.g. hospitals.
- Ensure all antennae are at least 20 cm from all persons.
- Ensure any high gain, wall or mast mount antennae are professionally installed and at least 30 cm from all persons.

Quick Test
Discuss the major influences on wireless LAN design.

Section 7: End of chapter assessment

Questions

1. Outline the five design goals that must be taken into consideration when undertaking a network design.

2. Discuss how the positioning of networking devices and equipment is fundamental to good network design.

3. There are four basic steps in network design methodology. Name these four steps and discuss each.

4. Discuss the process of capacity planning and outline how you would undertake this process for an organisation.

5. Prove that the figures shown below provide startup time of almost 21 minutes and an average hourly load of 2.5 Mbps:
   - 25 computers;
   - 30 MB software;
   - 10 MB data (both software and data must be downloaded before the machines can be used);
   - 1 hour time slot;
   - 10Base2 networking.

   Rerun the above example to show that the same load can be handled by 100BaseT in less than two minutes.

6. Discuss the major considerations of wireless LAN design and outline their importance when designing a wireless LAN.

Answers

1. To answer this question you need to name and discuss briefly the five main goals of network design: functionality, scalability, adaptability, manageability and availability. You need to demonstrate that you understand the importance of each of the terms to the process of network design. Remember these represent the goals of network design.

2. This question requires you to demonstrate your knowledge about the positioning of networking devices. You should discuss why the positioning of networking devices is critical to the best performance of the network. You should also discuss what the two types of server are, and what is meant by the terms 'collision' and 'broadcast domains'. Ideally, you should illustrate your answer with diagrams that show the correct placement of both workgroup and organisational servers. You should also give examples of how the correct positioning of the various types of networking devices will create collision and broadcast domains and explain the expected benefits of this.

3. This question is in two parts. The first asks you to name the four basic steps in network design methodology. This serves as a guide to help you structure the rest of the question, but you will gain marks for simply naming them. The second part asks you to discuss each of the steps. There is plenty to discuss and so you should plan your answer carefully so you don't run out of time. You should ensure you explain that this is a sequential procedure and you should stress the importance of gathering all the facts and of correct analysis and design. Most network designers scrimp on the documentation, which is bad practice – especially when 80% of all network problems occur at layer one. You should stress the importance of good documentation and its value when something goes wrong.

4. The important thing to note about this question is that it is asking you not only to discuss the process of capacity planning, but also to embellish your answer by discussing how you would undertake capacity planning for an organisation. You need to discuss the four steps in the process of capacity planning, detailing the figures you need to calculate the current and required load. You should identify the timespan under consideration – the example in the chapter had a one-hour interval. You also need to discuss how you would determine if there is enough capacity in the network to cope with both peak loads and the daily/session requirements.

The assessor would not expect you to undertake the maths, but would expect an explanation of how you would determine the current and required capacity, both for peak times and for the daily load.

5. This question is very specific. The assessor is asking you to calculate two types of capacity plan: one showing the length of time it will take for the machines to become operational (software and data to be loaded), the other showing the average load across the time period (1 hour). The formulae are given in the crucial concept box at the end of *Section 5*. The question also contains the answer and you are asked to prove it.

Time to start:

$$\frac{((25 \times ((10 \text{ MB} + 30 \text{ MB}) \times 8))\ 10\%) = 21 \text{ minutes}}{7 \text{ Mbps*}}$$

(*This should be replaced by 100 Mbps when re-running the calculation for 100BaseT.)

Average load:

$$\frac{((25 \times ((10 \text{ MB} + 30 \text{ MB}) \times 8))\ 10\%) = 2.5 \text{ Mbps}}{3600 \text{ seconds}}$$

The average load will be the same on 100BaseT as the network speed is not taken into account in this calculation.

6. This question is prompting you to show that you understand that wireless LAN design is more than simply installing an access point. The examiner is asking you to list the major considerations of LAN design and also asking you why they are important. You will probably get half of the marks from discussing the major considerations and the other half for giving reasons for their importance – make sure you answer both!

Section 9: Further reading and research

Cisco Networking Academy Program (2004) *CCNA 1 and 2 Companion Guide* (3rd edn). Cisco Press. ISBN: 1 58713 150 1. Chapter 5.

Chapter 8

Network software

Chapter summary

This chapter is the first of three that look at the role, setup and management of a typical network server. The hardware and software that comprise network facilitate the exchange of data and applications. Perhaps the most important piece of hardware is the server. Most organisations deploy either a Windows-based server or a UNIX-based server. Here we will concentrate on UNIX, for two main reasons:

● UNIX provides greater scalability and is therefore used in large organisations.

● A public domain version of UNIX (Linux) is available which will enable you to practise installing a networked operating system at a low cost.

Learning outcomes

After studying this chapter you should aim to test your achievement of the following outcomes. You should be able to:

Outcome 1: Multi-user operating systems

Understand the main features of multi-user, multi-tasking operating systems. Question 1 at the end of this chapter will test you on this.

Outcome 2: The UNIX filing structure

Understand the filing structure used in a UNIX filing system. Question 2 at the end of this chapter will test you on this.

Outcome 3: Filing system security

Understand and be able to manage security in a file server environment. Question 3 at the end of this chapter will test you on this.

How will you be assessed on this?

This subject area lends itself quite well to exam-type assessments rather than assignments. As there are many questions that could be asked about this subject, you should make sure you understand what is covered in this chapter well in advance of any examinations. You may also be assessed in your practical ability to setup a NOS.

Section 1: Multi-user operating systems

Computers that act as servers must be able to cope with the access demands of many different users and also be able to provide these users with the services they require. Servers vary in their capability to do this depending on the operating system that has been installed. UNIX enables users to access files and it also processes on their behalf. Multi-user operating systems also vary in the way in which jobs are given access to the processor. It is important you understand the basics of multi-user operating systems as these are important not only in the world of work, but also in the world of exams!

Peer-to-peer networks

As we have noted throughout this book, the whole point of networks is to facilitate the exchange of data and software. As we saw in *Chapter 1*, this exchange can be accomplished through peer-to-peer networking, such as Windows 98, 2000 and XP.

However, as noted earlier, peer-to-peer networks are only suitable for small networking situations. Once an organisation reaches the limit of its peer-to-peer network, it must consider installing a server.

Multi-user operating systems

Larger organisations or those that have outgrown a peer-to-peer network must make use of a server. As all the users will depend upon the performance of the machine chosen to be the server, the server's operating system must be suitable for multi-user tasking: it must be able to undertake more than one job at a time for more than one user at a time. UNIX is a good example of such an operating system as (and depending upon the hardware) it enables a tens of users each to have tens of jobs active at the same time.

Needless to say, multi-user, multi-tasking operating systems are extremely complex. They are responsible for such tasks as:

- job scheduling;
- the allocation of resources;
- hardware operations;
- user operations;
- protecting the user's work;
- protecting each user's working memory;
- providing disk storage and quotas for each user;
- running each user's various jobs.

Multi-user, multi-tasking operating systems can be classified into two groups, depending on the way jobs are given access to the processor.

Non-pre-emptive systems

Non-pre-emptive operating systems wait until a job quits the processor voluntarily. Should this job go into a loop and therefore not quit the processor, no other job will be allowed access to the processor. The server is thus hung and would need to be rebooted. Early versions of Novell Netware operated on this principle.

Pre-emptive systems

Pre-emptive operating systems are more complex. A job is given a time slice for access to the processor. If the job does not quit the processor voluntarily, it will be removed once its time slice is up. Even though it is given another time slice its access is suspended whilst other jobs have their turn on the processor. As this type of operating system is robust, a looping job will not take the processor down. It is also a fairer method of access as each job is given a turn without having to wait for the previous job(s) to finish. UNIX is an example of such a system.

> **KEY CONCEPT**
>
> Servers that offers pre-emptive scheduling afford greater resilience to rogue software.

Quick test

Briefly discuss the features you would expect from a multi-user, multi-tasking operating system.

Section 2: The UNIX filing structure

Multi-user operating systems have large and complex filing systems, and UNIX is no exception. UNIX can support a great many hard disks, and even many computers, inside its filing system. This means an entire organisation can be housed within one filing system. It is important to note, however, that a filing system on a large machine is not restricted to the size of its hard disk drive.

Directory structures

In DOS or Windows, the filing system is based on the physical disk drive – if there are two 40 GB disk drives these are assigned a drive identifier (e.g. drive C) and access to the information on these drives is obtained by using these letters. This system works quite well with filing systems that fit on to a physical drive but, in large multi-user systems, such a huge amount of data needs to be stored as it will not fit on one physical drive. Hence the filing system in UNIX is not drive based. Instead, there is one filing structure to embrace the entire filing system. This system might be the entire organisation, one department or even specific areas within one department. UNIX's filing system can span multiple physical disk drives or even multiple machines (*see Figure 8.1*).

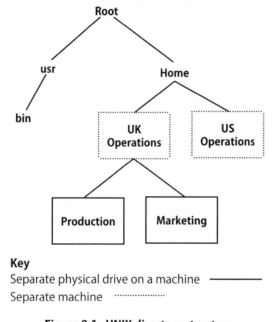

Key
Separate physical drive on a machine ————
Separate machine ··················

Figure 8.1: UNIX directory structure

This filing system is spread across three machines. The machine being accessed hosts the **/usr/bin** directory, whilst the home directory is split across two physical machines, one housing UK operations and the other US operations. It is possible for these machines to be located in their respective countries but still to provide access from one to the other. This is possible through the Networked Filing System (NFS) – a UNIX protocol that allows filing systems to be distributed, but yet accessible, throughout an entire network.

Many UNIX machines use the principle of logical volumes. Essentially, a logical volume is a way of joining two or more physical disks. For example, if a company has a corporate database of 120 GB but the only drives available are 80 GB. If this database must be contained on one disk only, there will be a problem. The solution is to create one logical volume spanning two physical drives (*Figure 8.2*). The database can then be saved to the logical volume rather than the physical disk (or volume).

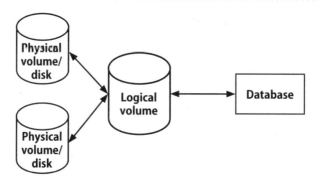

Figure 8.2: Logical volumes

Quick test

Briefly discuss the UNIX filing system, highlighting the differences between this system and a filing system you are familiar with.

Section 3: Filing system security

Users and groups

When multiple users have access to a filing system, individual users' files must be protected. For instance, the managing director of a company would not be pleased if all the staff had access to the personnel records. To provide this protection, UNIX uses the idea of file owners and groups: access permissions can be set for both owners and groups. In this way, the UNIX filing systems can provide file protection and security. The files stored on a UNIX machine can belong to any user. However, some files will be confidential whilst others will require wider access – perhaps to project groups or even everyone on the system. For example, a company intranet should be accessible to everyone in the organisation, but budgetary information might be restricted to senior management. Using the principle of file owners and groups, UNIX supports such access, and *Figure 8.3* shows a directory listing where the owner of the file (**cs0pir**) and the group to which the file belongs (staff) have been highlighted.

```
$ ls -lisa|more
total 6963
    7324902     2 -rw-------1  cs0pir staff      25 Mar 23 11:53 #fred#
    7324800     8 drwx-x-x 46  cs0pir staff      3584 May 30 12:30 .
    7324817     2 lrwxrwxrwx 1  cs0pir staff      36 Mar 23 11:52 .#fred ->
cs0pir@isis.sunderland.ac.uk.16165:1
            2 1 dr-xr-xr-x 21 root root       21 May 30 12:51 ..
    7324877     2 -rw-r-r- 1  cs0pir staff      446 Jun 27 1997 .ab_library
    7324882     2 -rw-r-r- 1  cs0pir staff      141 Jun 27 1997 .ab_library.lock
    7328640     2 drwxr-xr-x 2  cs0pir staff      512 Sep 23 1994 .cetables
    7324804     2 -rw-r-r- 1  cs0pir staff      747 Mar 8 1996 .cshrc
```

Figure 8.3: Users and groups

The systems administrator is usually a superuser (the root account in UNIX). The superuser has unrestricted privileges and access to all files and directories (the superuser account is used in *Chapter 9* to set up a UNIX system).

Rights

To the left of the owner and group information in *Figure 8.3* is information about the file's rights. For example:

-rwxr–r-x

The first character denotes that it is either a file (-), a directory (d) or a link (l). The following three characters represent the owner's rights – in this case **rwx** indicating that the user has read, write and execute permissions to the file. The second group of three characters represents the rights of the group – in this case members of the group this file belongs to can only read the file. The final three characters represent the rights of the rest of the world – in this case, read and execute.

To change the permissions, the systems administrator or the file's owner uses the **chmod** command. There are essentially two ways of using this command, but the easiest and most common way is to use the following criteria to determine the value of the rights to be added and then to use the command below to add them:

Right required	Value
Read	4
Write	2
Execute (search if the target is a directory)	1

chmod abc <filename>

In this command, a indicates the rights of the owner, b the rights of the group and c the rights of the rest of the world. To allocate more than one right, the values are simply added together: for read and execute this is 4 + 1 = 5. Thus the command to give all rights to all users would be **chmod 777 <filename>**. For web pages, **chmod 755 *** is normally used. This gives the owner **rwx**, the group r-x and the rest of the world r-x to all files in that directory (* is the wildcard mask). Rights can be applied equally to both files and directories. Ownership of the file can usually only be changed by the systems administrator through the use of the **chown** command; the group can be changed by the systems administrator or the owner using the **chgrp** command (*Figure 8.4*).

mainserve:/home/phil/crucial/test % ls -l
total 2
-rw-------1phil staff 69 Nov22 16:57 myfile
mainserve:/home/phil/crucial/test % chgrp student myfile
mainserve:/home/phil/crucial/test % ls -l
total 2
-rw-------1phil student 69 Nov22 16:57 myfile
mainserve:/home/phil/crucial/test %

Figure 8.4: Changing groups

Inherited rights

For even tighter security, it is possible to set default rights that are given to a file upon its creation. Known as inherited rights, this is achieved using the **umask** command in UNIX. The major advantage of using such a command is that it removes the need for the user to ensure that the file is appropriately protected. However, care must be taken that such files are not made accessible to the group or the world by accident. This can be quite difficult for an inexperienced user.

The **umask** command sets the default permissions given to newly created files. The first digit defines the rights value to be subtracted from the owner permissions (which cannot be modified). The following two digits define the rights of the group and the world, respectively. Thus the command **umask 077** does not alter the rights of the owner but removes all the rights of the group and the world. The command **umask 022** removes write access from the group and the world. *Figure 8.5* shows an example of the **umask** command in operation.

```
$
$ umask
022
$ date > date.txt
$ ls -l date.txt
-rw-r–r– 1 phil staff        34 Apr 26 11:34 date.txt
$ umask 077
$ date > date2.txt
$ls -l dat*.*
-rw-r–r– 1 phil staff        34 Apr 26 11:34 date.txt
-rw-------1phil staff        34 Apr26 11:34 date2.txt
$
```

Figure 8.5: The umask command in operation

Setting up security on files and directories

The file owner and group commands form the heart of file system security in the UNIX operating system. The operating system checks the access rights of a user who is trying to access a file and allows only the access specified. It is, however, also possible to combine the directory permissions and the file permissions to increase security. For example, by removing the read attributes from a directory, it is possible to prevent users from seeing the contents of the directory they are accessing. To access this directory, the user must specify the entire path and the filename. In *Figure 8.6*, the contents of the test2 directory can be listed but, in the shaded line, all rights except execute have been removed. The owner can now only list the files if he or she knows the entire path and the filename.

```
mainserve:/home/phil/crucial/test % ls -l
total 2
drwxr-xr-x 2 phil staff       512 Nov 22 17:02 test2
mainserve:/home/phil/crucial/test % ls -l test2
total 2
-rw-------1phil staff         111Nov 22 17:04 myfile
mainserve:/home/phil/crucial/test % chmod 100 test2
mainserve:/home/phil/crucial/test % ls -l test2
test2: Permission denied
total 2
mainserve:/home/phil/crucial/test % cat ./test2/myfile
This is a really quick test to show you how files can be protected by altering the attributes of the directory.
mainserve:/home/phil/crucial/test %
```

Figure 8.6: Protecting a file by disallowing directory listings

Other file and directory attributes

In addition to the file attributes given above, UNIX also has attributes for hidden and compressed files.

In UNIX, files are hidden in rather an odd fashion – the filename is preceded by a full stop (.). Thus such files as **.profile**, **.chsrc**, etc., aren't seen when a simple directory-listing command is used (**ls -l**). To see these files, the **-a** (all argument) command must be used. Files that are compressed in UNIX are given the extension **.z**. Thus **myfile.z** is a compressed version of **myfile**.

Quick test
Briefly outline how files are protected in the UNIX operating system.

Section 4: End of chapter assessment

Questions

1. Discuss the main features of a multi-user operating system.

2. Discuss how the filing structure of a typical multi-user machine, UNIX, is organised.

3. Discuss how filing system security is achieved in the UNIX operating system. Wherever possible, illustrate your answers with examples or commands.

Answers

1. To answer this question, you need to demonstrate your knowledge of multi-user operating system features. Although the question doesn't call for a direct comparison, it is worth mentioning that a multi-user operating system is much more complex than smaller, peer-to-peer ones. You should also mention the functions a multi-user operating system needs to provide and should discuss the two types of scheduling. You should mention the fact that these two types of scheduling are very important as they determine the server's resilience to rogue software.

2. Here you need to discuss the organisation of UNIX's filing system. Your answer should be put into context by mentioning the fact that, because UNIX is a multi-user operating system, the files of individual users must be protected – unlike, say, desktop Windows or DOS. You must discuss the fact that the directory structure in a UNIX environment is not disk based but directory based, which means that it is not limited to the size or location of a physical disk drive or even a machine. It is always worth using a diagram to illustrate your answer.

3. To answer this question, you need to discuss how filing system security is implemented in UNIX. You need to discuss the fact that filing system security in UNIX centres on the idea of file owner, file group and the rest of the world, and that permissions for access can be granted or revoked from either or all on a controlled basis. You should discuss how such access is granted and, if possible, illustrate your answer with the required commands. Some discussion of how the security may be increased further (using inherited rights) is also extremely worthwhile.

Section 5: Further reading and research

Afzal, A. (2002) *UNIX Unbounded: A Beginning Approach.* Prentice Hall. ISBN: 0 13092 836 8. Section 2.

Chapter 9

Setting up a networked operating system

Chapter summary

The correct installation of a networked operating system is critical – NOSs must be very reliable and readily available, a poor setup can jeopardise this. This chapter sets out the basics of the most common tasks involved in setting up a networked operating system:

- Installing and configuring a networked operating system.

- Creating a suitable user environment.

- Managing printer services.

However, there is not the space here to cover everything you need to know to setup and configure a networked operating system; this is meant as a guide only.

Learning outcomes

After studying this chapter you should aim to test your achievement of the following outcomes. You should be able to:

Outcome 1: Installing and configuring Linux and its applications
Understand the steps involved in configuring a typical NOS and in installing an application. Question 1 at the end of this chapter will test you on this.

Outcome 2: Configuring the user environment
Understand the need for, and be able to configure, the end-user environment. Question 2 at the end of this chapter will test you on this.

Outcome 3: Printer setup and options
Understand the issues involved with the installation and maintenance of printers. Question 3 at the end of this chapter will test you on this.

How will you be assessed on this?

Assessment in this area is not straightforward. Ideally, an assessor would like to see a student install an operating system successfully. However, pressures of time often mean they are forced to ask students to prepare a guide that will allow anyone to install an operating system. You may also be asked to establish groups, to add users and add these users to groups. You may well be tested on your understanding of this in an exam or TCT.

Section 1: Installing Linux and applications

Networked operating systems (NOS) are complex pieces of software and need careful installation and management. For the purposes of this chapter, Linux's **Fedora Core 4** will be installed. However, this is a general installation guide for **Fedora Core 4** – this installation cannot cover every possible user configuration. A PC is one of the most complicated computers available – a trip to a local PC shop will demonstrate the vast range of equipment available (e.g. CD-ROMs, DVDs, scanners, processors, memory, etc.). This vast array of products means that just about every PC is different. This makes the installation of a complex operating system such as Linux difficult – there are so many choices. Whilst this is a general guide, it is strongly recommended you visit Fedora's website (**www.fedora.redhat.com**) where you will find many installation manuals and a great deal of information about installing Linux. This chapter covers a new and full installation.

> ## TIPS & ADVICE
> Installing Linux can be a very painful experience. One of the best ways of avoiding this is to select a powerful version of Linux that is renowned for its ease of installation. I found Fedora Core to be one of the easiest to install.

Installation process

> ## WARNING !
> This process may well destroy applications or data resident on a computer system. Proceed with caution and, preferably, use a machine at university or college that has been allocated for such use.

First steps

Fedora Core is undoubtedly one of the easiest versions of Linux to install. The best way of installing is to access the BIOS settings of the machine and then set it to boot from the CD drive – make sure the BIOS settings are saved. Next, the first installation disk should be inserted into the CD-ROM drive and the machine rebooted. The initial Fedora screen appears (*Figure 9.1*).

Figure 9.1: Initial Fedora Core screen

127

Testing media

Fedora now asks if you want to verify the media (the installation CD). If you are sure the media is good, then you can skip this (*Figure 9.2*). You are now presented with the Fedora Core welcome screen – click **Next** to begin installation and select the language.

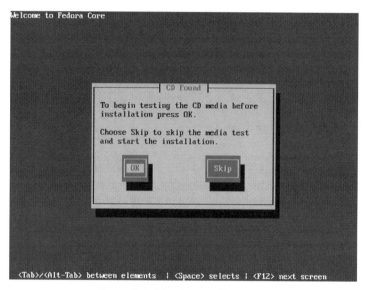

Figure 9.2: Testing media screen

Language selection

You are now presented with the **Language Selection** screen (*Figure 9.3*). Language selection is obviously important; it will affect all system documentation. Select the appropriate language and click **Next**. You will now be asked for keyboard type. Select the appropriate keyboard (e.g. United Kingdom) and click **Next**.

Figure 9.3: Language selection screen

Upgrade/install

Fedora may ask whether you want to update an existing version or install a fresh. Select install and click **Next**.

Installation type

Fedora now asks for the **Installation Type** (*Figure 9.4*). Choose the correct installation type for your situation.

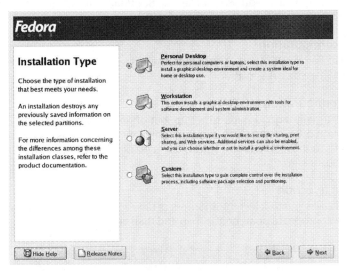

Figure 9.4: Choosing the installation type

Automatic partitioning

Fedora now needs to set up a partition (to store data and applications) and it gives you various options as to where data will be stored and what will be removed. Unless you have good reason, select auto (*Figure 9.5*). Fedora now asks you to confirm your choices.

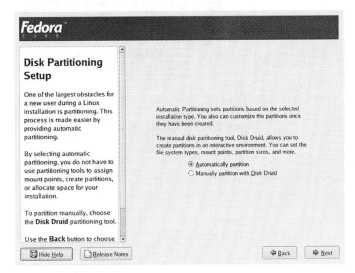

Figure 9.5: Automatic partitioning

Bootloader

Fedora now asks where you would like the **Bootloader** installing – bootloader is a manager for boot up. It is best to accept defaults.

Network configuration

At this point Fedora asks you to configure the network. Again, it is recommended to accept defaults, which is DHCP.

Firewall configuration

A firewall is usually a good thing to set up, but often with Linux it makes carrying out the installation process, installing packages and connecting users a little more tricky. It is best not to configure the firewall until you have completed the installation – it can be turned on post-installation.

Time zone selection

Next, Fedora asks you to select the appropriate time zone – you should simply be able to click on the appropriate point on the map and then click **Next** (*Figure 9.6*).

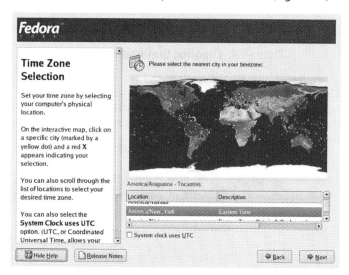

Figure 9.6: Time zone selection

Root password

Root is the superuser of the UNIX system – essentially it's God. The root password must be protected and forgetting the password could mean reinstallation and loss of data. However, the root password must not be written down if at all possible: this would compromise the system. The password is not displayed on the screen and it will be requested twice. Enter the root password, confirm the password and click **Next** to continue.

Fedora now summarises this information. If it is correct, click **Next** to continue.

Package installation

Fedora now asks which packages you wish to install (based upon your earlier selection in the **Installation Type** screen). Again, normally accepting the default is recommended (*Figure 9.7*) – further packages can be added later.

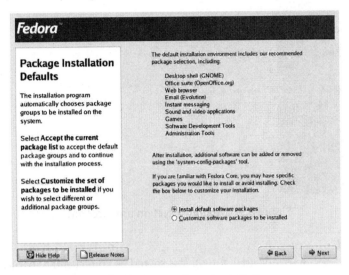

Figure 9.7: The Fedora package installation screen

Installing

Fedora now begins installation – this can take some time.

Installation complete

Once installation is complete, remove the CD from the CD-drive and then click on **Reboot** to reboot the system.

Post-installation tasks

One of the first post-installation tasks is to accept the licence agreement. Next, the system time and date need to be verified/entered.

Display

Fedora now asks you to verify the display settings. If correct, click **Next** to continue.

User accounts

You are prompted to create a system user – this is the first (non administrative) user of the system. Enter details (*Figure 9.8*) and click **Next** to continue.

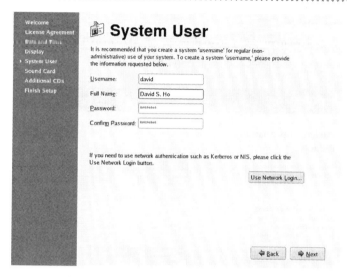

Figure 9.8: Creating a system user account

Soundcard

Fedora will detect a soundcard (if fitted). This should be correct and if so, click **Next** to continue.

Additional software

At this point additional software on further CDs can be installed (if necessary).

Installing applications

Further applications can be added after install by selecting desktop from the menu then **Add/Remove** applications (*Figure 9.9*).

Figure 9.9: Adding and removing applications

Adding users and groups

Adding users and groups is a relatively straightforward task in Linux. **Select Desktop** > **System Settings** > **Users and Groups** (*Figure 9.10*).

Figure 9.10: Configuring users and groups

You are then presented with the **User Manager** screen (*Figure 9.11*).

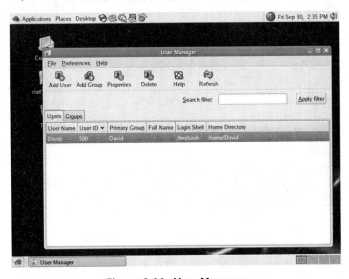

Figure 9.11: User Manager

Click on the **Add User** button. In this window, you can specify user name (*Figure 9.12*).

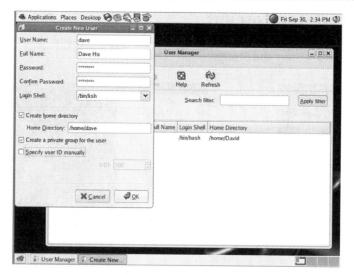

Figure 9.12: Create New User

To add a group, click on the **Add Group** button from **User Manager**. You will be presented with the **Create New Group** window (*Figure 9.13*).

Figure 9.13: Creating a new group

Enter the name of the group and click on **OK**. The group is now created. Users can be added to the group by returning to the **Properties** section of **User Manger** and selecting **Groups** (*Figure 9.14*).

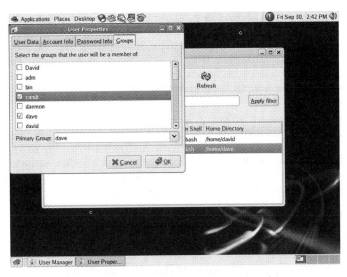

Figure 9.14: Selecting group membership

You should select their primary group and any secondary groups required. Deleting users and groups or removing users from groups can be achieved in a similar fashion.

KEY CONCEPT

The correct installation of Linux is the key to the success of the operating system. Therefore, when installing the operating system, ensure you make the right choices.

Quick test

Briefly outline the steps involved in installing a version of Linux.

Section 2: Configuring the user environment

Once a NOS is installed, the user environment normally needs to be configured. Configuration includes allocating users to a group, giving users access to the facilities of that group, creating login scripts to set the users' environment and, possibly, creating menu scripts to tighten security and to make the system easier to use.

User environment

As standard, UNIX provides two types of user environment – a command line interface (CLI), which is a text-driven interface similar to DOS, and a graphical user interface (GUI) similar to Windows. Which is chosen is a matter of personal choice and environmental conditions. If using a UNIX machine, you will be able to use the GUI but, if working remotely (e.g. through the Internet), you would use the CLI. Both interfaces will give access to files and will provide the user with full access to the server.

One of the most popular ways of using a UNIX server is to implement Windows as the desktop operating system and to configure it to use UNIX as the server. For files, this can be achieved quite easily by setting Windows to use a remote drive, which should be configured as NFS. NFS (Networked File System), as we saw in *Chapter 8*, allows UNIX to share its filing system over a network. NFS is also available on Windows-based machines. Other applications (such as Oracle), tend to work in one of two ways. The first is as a piece of software installed locally (in the case of Oracle, SQL*Net) that allows applications on the PC to access the database on the server. For example, a list of all students' names and email addresses might be required in an Excel spreadsheet. By using the appropriate software, a query can be built in Excel that will then be sent to the Oracle database on UNIX. The UNIX-based software will then process the query and return the required list into the spreadsheet. In this example, the UNIX machine is behaving as a true server – it is using its immense processing power to retrieve the required data to send to the PC.

The second popular way of accessing a server is through a web-based interface. As web pages and dynamic web pages develop, it is becoming possible to provide end users with an interface to an application that is held centrally on the server. Using the server in this way means an increased load on the server but, at the same time, the PCs need less power. As this technology continues to develop, scripts written in Java will be executable on a PC, thus reducing the server's workload.

User interfaces

GUIs provide the end-user with a point-and-click environment in which they can control and run their applications. Multi-user GUIs have extensions that allow them to deal with file access privileges. They also have an interface that permits the management of quite complex activities (providing the user has the rights of access to them), such as adding a user, a group or a device.

The real power of a UNIX server, however, comes in the form of the CLI. In the CLI, commands are submitted to the operating system via a **shell**. A shell is an environment that allows commands to be issued (like DOS), and it also has facilities to control input, output and programming facilities that allow complex sets of actions to be performed. A unique feature of the CLI in UNIX is that there are many to choose from. The user is able to select the 'shell' that best matches his or her experience and current needs. These shells are incredibly powerful and have a programming language of their own. One of the most common and powerful general-purpose shells is the Korn shell.

As with DOS, it is possible to place commands that would normally be keyed in at the command line into a file. This file can then be given execute permission and executed. Such a file (containing UNIX shell commands) is known as a **script** (or shell script). Executing the script is equivalent to keying in the commands within it. UNIX shells are quite sophisticated programming languages in their own right, and there are entire books devoted to programming in them. Together with the large number of special utility programs provided as standard, scripts make UNIX an extremely powerful operating system: they provide UNIX with an extensive programming language and an extremely flexible environment for controlling and configuring users.

Login scripts

Login scripts are similar to the **autoexec.bat** and the **config.sys** files of Windows/DOS except that, in a multi-user environment, they work on a per-user basis rather than on a machine basis. Thus, whenever a user logs on to a UNIX machine, his or her environment is configured automatically. Such things as the preferred editor or printer are set and, in the case of systems that use KDE or CDE graphical desktop environments, the preferred Windows settings are also set. Login scripts in UNIX vary depending upon the shell in use. Each shell has a different startup file, which provides flexibility when configuring the environment. The file's name depends upon the default shell in use – UNIX has different names, one for each shell. The one for the Korn shell is known as .profile (it will be remembered from the last chapter that the . at the front causes the file to be hidden).

Figure 9.14 shows a default .profile script. The lines that begin with a # are comment lines. The fourth line will print the phrase 'Hello Im running .profile' to the screen. Line 5 is interesting. It sets up an alias to allow the user to run the UNIX command **ls -lisa** by keying in **dir**. Line 6 sets the working path, and line 7 makes the working path usable.

Line 8 sets the type of terminal in use as a virtual terminal (VT) type 100.

```
$ cat .profile|more
#          This is the default standard profile provided to a user.
#          They are expected to edit it to meet their own needs.

echo Hello Im running .profile
alias dir="ls -lisa"
PATH=$OPENWINHOME/bin:$OPENWINHOME/lib:$ORACLE_HOME/lib
export PATH
TERM=vt100;export TERM
```

Figure 9.14: Default .profile script

Menu systems

Often, administrators will want to make the system easy to use and may also want to increase security – if the end-users are not allowed access to the operating system commands, they can do a great deal less damage both by accident and maliciously. The script in *Figure 9.15* provides the end-user with a menu system. The user can choose to get the date, the current directory, a directory listing or can exit. Sample output is shown in *Figure 9.16*. By inserting a call to this script (together with the UNIX trap command) into the user's .profile file, the administrator is able to control what the user is and is not able to do. The trap command traps break commands (e.g. control-c), which prevents the user from breaking out of the menu. *Figure 9.17* shows the revised .profile (including the trap command).

```
$cat menu
#!/bin/ksh
#Simple menu script written by P J Irving 3/9/02
select REPLY in "System Date" "Current Directory" "Directory Listing" "Exit"
do
        case $REPLY in
                "System Date")
                        date
                        ;;
                "Current Directory")
                        pwd
                        ;;
                "Directory Listing")
                        ls -l
                        ;;
                "Exit")
                        break
                        ;;
                *)
                        echo "I do not recognise your choice"
                        ;;
        esac
done
```

Figure 9.15: Simple menu script

```
$ menu
1) System Date
2) Current Directory
3) Directory Listing
4) Exit
#? 1
Tuesday September 9 18:25:31 BST 2002
#? 2
/home/phil/unixbook
#? 3 total 2
-rwx------1phil staff        354 Apr 27 18:20 menu
#? 8
I do not recognise your choice
1) System Date
2) Current Directory
3) Directory Listing
4) Exit
#? 4
$
```

Figure 9.16: Sample output from the script in *Figure 9.15*

```
$cat .profile|more
#          This is the default standard profile provided to a user.
#          They are expected to edit it to meet their own needs.
echo Hello Im running .profile
alias dir="ls -lisa"
PATH=$OPENWINHOME/bin:$OPENWINHOME/lib:$ORACLE_HOME/lib
export PATH
TERM=vt100;export TERM
tap 'echo you cant use ctrl=-c' INT
menu
```

Figure 9.17: Revised .profile script (note the trap command)

KEY CONCEPT

Menus are very useful. They provide the user with limited choice and therefore limited functionality within the system. They are very powerful when combined with login scripts, the break command allowing the user to undertake the tasks on the menu without accessing the operating system. This increases internal security.

Quick test

Briefly outline how shell scripts in the UNIX environment can help to make the server secure.

Section 3: Printer setup and options

NOSs tend to have many different printers that are often located in users' offices . It is important, therefore, that both the printer and the queue are set up correctly and that user output is directed to the correct printer (this is usually done in the user configuration file – see Section 2).

Setting up the printer

The following are general points concerning the attachment of printers. Printers can be attached to UNIX systems in a variety of ways: they can be attached directly to the computer system via serial or parallel ports; they can be attached via printer server units networked to the UNIX machine; and some workstations provide for the direct connection of a printer.

When installing a printing device, that device's use must be considered carefully. If the printer is to print on secure stationery (e.g. cheques), it must be secured both physically and logically. Logical security is necessary to remove the threat of someone printing a cheque with their name on. Indeed, if a printer contains anything other than blank paper it will probably need to be controlled. Pre-printed order forms could be open to fraudulent use, as could invoices, credit notes, etc. Even letter-headed stationery needs to be protected in some way – it is relatively expensive and can be wasted if used for program listings, etc.

In general, printers are found in the /dev directory and have the following attributes:

Device name	Description
/dev/lp0	First parallel printer
/dev/lp1	Second parallel printer
/dev/lp2	Third parallel printer

Serial printers are assigned to serial devices (e.g. **/dev/ttyS0** for the first serial printer, **/dev/ttyS1** for the second, and so on).

Printing options

To support multi-user access, printer functions are extended in UNIX. The basic print command is **lp** or **lpr** (an abbreviation for line printer), followed by the filename (e.g. **lp myfile** would queue the file myfile for later printing). Often users wish to check the status of printing, perhaps to determine the position of their print job in the queue. This can be achieved using the **lpq** command. When using the lpq command, each entity in the queue has a unique job number. Should a user wish to remove a job from the queue, he or she needs to know this job number (*see below*).

It is usual for a multi-user system to have several printers connected to it and, providing he or she has permission, the user can select whichever printer he or she wishes to use for a job. This is achieved by using the **–p** switch in the **lp** command. Thus **lp –p printer filename** will cause the file named to be printed on the printer named. Status check and job cancellation also support the **–p** switch.

Managing printer queues

In most cases, all printers can be seen and managed by the systems administrator. Printers in UNIX usually need little management other than 'standard' maintenance (toner, ribbons, paper, etc.). Occasionally, jobs need to be removed from the print queue, which can be done by a user (providing he or she owns the job). System administrator privilege is only necessary when the owner of a job is not available and his or her job requires attention. *Table 9.1* provides a summary of printer maintenance commands.

Command	Description	Example
lpstat printer	Displays information about the current status of the LP print service	lpstat –o all
lpq	Displays the status of jobs on the printer specified	lpq –p stuprinter
lprm	Cancels printing of the specified job	lprm 123

Table 9.1: Printer maintenance commands

The **lpq** command, if used without any parameters, displays information about the default printer's queue. When used with the **–p** switch this allows a particular printer name to be specified, and it provides the following information:

- print job ID;
- the owner of the job;
- the name of the file being printed;
- the size of the file.

The **lprm** command can be used to remove jobs from the print queue. Again, the default printer's queue will be accessed unless another printer name is specified. There are two ways of using the **lprm** command – to remove specified jobs from the queue or to remove all jobs from the queue.

To remove particular files, the job's ID must be established (using the lpq command). To remove job 321, **lprm 321** would be keyed in. Care must be taken when typing lprm as lprm on its own will remove all the jobs from the default printer's queues. To remove jobs from a specific printer queue, **lprm -queuename** should be used, where **queuename** is the name of the queue to be cleared.

Many variants of UNIX have specific commands for printer management (for instance, IBM/HP/SCO/Solaris, etc., use **lpadmin** for the general administration of printers and cancel for cancelling print jobs).

> **KEY CONCEPT**
>
> Managing printers in Linux means being responsible not only for your own work, but also for that of others. Print queues allow users to send their jobs for printing where they will queue until it is their turn on the printer.

> **TIPS & ADVICE**
>
> Most of these commands have GUI equivalents.

Quick test

Briefly discuss how print jobs are managed, using the command line in Linux.

Section 4: End of chapter assessment

Questions

1. Outline the major steps involved in installing Linux.

2. *Figure 9.18* shows a shell script. Briefly discuss what the shell script does, annotating this example with appropriate comments, and provide a sample output. Discuss why such scripts are very useful for security.

```
$cat menu
#!/bin/ksh
select REPLY in "System Date" "Current Directory" "Directory Listing" "Exit"
do
        case $REPLY in
        "System Date")
                date
                ;;
        "Current Directory")
                pwd
                ;;
        "Directory Listing")
        ls -l
                ;;
        "Exit")
                break
                ;;
        *)
                echo "I do not recognise your choice"
                ;;
        esac
done
```

Figure 9.18: Sample shell script

3. Briefly discuss how printers are managed in the UNIX operating system.

Answers

1   To be fair, such a question is unlikely in an exam or TCT. You are far more likely to be asked either to install a version of Linux or to produce a user guide on the installation of Linux. In the latter case, you should note your intended audience and ensure that the language and style used are appropriate for this audience. Ultimately, the assessors are seeking to establish whether you can install a multi-user operating system, and the production of a manual gives them something that can be handed to the external examiner as proof of your abilities.

2.   Rather than being cruel and asking you to write a shell script in an exam or TCT, the assessor will often give you a shell script and ask you to annotate it with comments and give a sample output. This is a less painful way of ensuring you understand scripts. In this case, the script is a menu system that allows the user to call on a number of utilities. When it is executed it will present the output shown in *Figure 9.19*. You should annotate the shell script with appropriate comments. Remember, the assessor is not looking for comments such as 'this line prints out'; he or she is looking for a deeper understanding – for example, 'this section of the script traps and processes an invalid user input'. Finally, you need to identify why menus are so important to security in an operating system. Your answer to this question should ideally include the trap command being used in the shell's startup file.

> $ menu
> 1) System Date
> 2) Current Directory
> 3) Directory Listing
> 4) Exit
> #? 1
> Tuesday September 9 18:25:31 BST 2002
> #? 2
> /home/phil/unixbook
> #? 3
> total 2
> -rwx------1phil staff 354Apr 27 18:20menu
> #? 8
> I do not recognise your choice
> 1) System Date
> 2) Current Directory
> 3) Directory Listing
> 4) Exit
> #? 4

Figure 9.19: Sample output from question 2

3.   To answer this question you need to need to highlight the issues associated with printer management, list the commands used for printer management, discuss the function of each command and give an appropriate example of each command's use.

Section 5: Further reading and research

Afzal, A. (2002) *UNIX Unbounded: A Beginning Approach.* Prentice Hall ISBN: 0 13092 736 8. Section 2.

www.fedora.redhat.com

Chapter 10

Network management

Chapter summary

Managing a network is extremely important. There is a myth that once a network is installed it will virtually run itself. For all but the very simplest of networks, this is simply not the case. Today's networks are highly complex and often mission critical to organisations: they cannot be treated piecemeal – to perform well they must be managed and managed well. This chapter provides an introduction to network management. Of all management tasks, it is the backup that is the most important. This is reflected in its treatment in this chapter.

Learning outcomes

After studying this chapter you should aim to test your achievement of the following outcomes. You should be able to:

Outcome 1: Creating users and groups

Create users and groups and understand the security implications. Question 1 at the end of this chapter will test you on this.

Outcome 2: Managing networks

Understand how to manage networks in a proactive fashion to provide high-availability. Question 2 at the end of this chapter will test you on this.

Outcome 3: Security

Understand the need for network and system security, be able to evaluate security and devise, implement and monitor security policies. Question 3 at the end of this chapter will test you on this.

How will you be assessed on this?

The subject matter of this chapter is a blend of both practice and theory (although the theory is very practically focused!) and is likely to be assessed as such. As time is often tight in modules and resources are limited, it is likely your assessor will ask you to write a user manual detailing how to undertake the practical aspects. Such topics as backup and security lend themselves very well to exams and TCTs.

Section 1: Creating users and groups

One of the most common breaches of security in NOS is the creation of fictitious user and group accounts through which fraudulent transactions can be made.

Therefore, whilst this section deals with the process of creating users and groups, it also outlines the management procedures necessary to maintain security.

Creating users and groups

When establishing a UNIX system for the first time, careful consideration must be given to groups and their members. Most organisations have distinct groups (e.g. human resources, finance, manufacturing, etc.) that would naturally form UNIX groups. However, the nature of the information stored on the system dictates that groups must be selected carefully. For instance, not everyone in finance should have access to the printer containing cheques and, if everyone has access to the purchase order system, fraudulent purchase orders or invoices could be created. Thus user needs should be discussed carefully and user IDs should be created in an accountable and controlled fashion. Control Issues are usually dealt with by the human resources manager or head of the relevant department, and these people should detail the access levels required clearly. System administrators should grant only the minimum access necessary.

Similarly, when employees leave a company, the human resources department needs to inform the systems administrator, who should then suspend the user account. All memos sent by the human resources department should be kept by the systems administrator as confirmation for audit purposes. The accounts should be suspended rather than deleted, which leaves a trail for subsequent system auditing. Any changes to user accounts also need to have an audit trail. For example, if the head of purchasing wants a user to have access to the purchase order system, a memo should be sent to the systems administrator asking for this to be done. Simply acting on verbal information could place the administrator in a precarious position if there was a fraudulent incident.

This type of user management varies according to the organisation. For example, universities manage huge numbers of accounts for both staff and students. At the end of each academic year, roughly one third of all student accounts will cease and, at the beginning of the academic year, a new batch of accounts will be created. At the University of Sunderland there are approximately 12,000 students requiring approximately 4000 accounts to be created each September.

Different methods can be used to automate the creation of accounts, particularly in UNIX, but the accounts must still be created in a controlled way. Accounts represent the basic level of access to the network and the computer system. One possible solution for a university is to create user accounts from the registration system – a file could be downloaded from the registration system and processed via UNIX scripts to create an account. As each student in the registration system is a valid student, this process is safe. Standard student rights would also be given, as would standard passwords – perhaps a date of birth or some other code the students choose at the time of registration.

> **KEY CONCEPT**
>
> Control must be exercised over the creation of users. Creating users in an ad hoc fashion may well compromise the system.

Management of users

Once the process of creating accounts is complete, administrators need to be aware that a higher workload will follow from the increased number of users. Management of users, therefore, tends to fall into one of two categories:

- normal user management; and

- exceptional user management.

Normal users are the users systems administrators would expect to deal with each day – requests for help with a forgotten password, more disk storage space, printer problems, etc. Obviously, the higher the number of users, the higher the workload from this category of users. As its name suggests, exceptional user management involves dealing with exceptional cases, and these might mean breaches of security. The network manager or systems administrator should be on the lookout for security breaches and should investigate accordingly. Security breaches can often be detected as long continuous logins – perhaps the user doesn't log out when leaving for lunch or in the evening. Logins after hours or from strange or unknown computers often indicate a security breach. Ideally, of course, this should be blocked by the organisation's security policy. Most operating systems have extensive facilities for monitoring security and for tracking users. For example, the who command in UNIX can show who is currently logged on to the system, whereas the last command gives details of previous logins. Although primitive tools, they are a useful starting point for tracking users and monitoring security.

The management of workgroups also tends to be exceptional. Occasionally, a user will be assigned to another workgroup, either alongside his or her current group or as a full transfer. Systems administrators need to ensure users are allocated to the correct groups using the **chgrp** command (*see Chapter 8*).

KEY CONCEPT

Users must be managed to keep the system healthy. Security is dependent upon good user management.

Quick test

Briefly discuss the issues involved in user management.

Section 2: Managing networks

As has been noted elsewhere, the installation of a network is only the beginning: the successful management of a network is paramount if it is to be a valuable asset to an organisation. Key tasks in managing a network are ensuring continuity and integrity through backups and ensuring continued functionality through the continuous monitoring of resource usage.

Estimating resource usage

Estimating resource usage is an important part of network management. The goals of such management are to detect trends arising from the use of the network and to use these trends to plan future upgrades. To identify trends accurately and to provide a benchmark for resolving problems, it is important to measure the network and its performance immediately after installation. Known as baselining, this process ideally measures the load on the network and the network's response time at each user's machine. Only when this information has been collected can meaningful comparisons be made if users complain of the network's performance.

TIPS & ADVICE

The system must be baselined. If not, there will be nothing to measure current performance against.

Other measurements that should be taken include disk usage and the disk filing system. These can be taken using the following commands:

- df

- du

df provides information on used and available disk space (in kilobytes), as shown in *Figure 10.1*; **du** provides information on the number of kilobytes allocated to each of the specified filenames, as shown in *Figure 10.2*.

Filesystem	kybytes	used	avail	capacity	Mounted on
/dev/staff1	17415	10900	6515	62%	/
/dev/staff2	20300	11000	9300	54%	/usr

Figure 10.1: Sample df output

```
$df $ du|more
2        ./.wastebasket
16       ./.cetables
2        ./.logs
2        ./.tt
46       ./sql/osaass
236      ./sql
2        ./.netscape/cache
264      ./.netscape
2        ./bupdir
6        ./copydir
6        ./BUPDIR
16       ./mydir
6        ./COPYDIR
130      ./Java
2        ./bin
1026     ./soar6
–More–
```

Figure 10.2: Sample du output

Both these commands provide essential information on the filing system. Should the filing system become full, serious problems will arise. This is particularly true if **/tmp** becomes full as all UNIX applications use this as a 'scratch' area. Careful monitoring of the system is essential if problems are to be avoided, and can only be undertaken if there is a baseline to measure from. The **/tmp** directory normally only contains temporary files and it is the only directory from which the administrator can safely delete files – other directories contain essential system files and should not be deleted. Applications also usually have directories that grow – for instance, an accounting package will have a directory that contains audit trails. The size of this directory will grow as each transaction is made in the accounting package. The systems administrator should ensure these directories have enough space for their required growth, but the administrator of the accounts package should ensure this directory is maintained and unnecessary files removed.

Measurements should be taken frequently and be recorded. The exact frequency depends upon the machine's usage and the disk quotas imposed on users, but once a week is normally sufficient. Measurements and backups must be taken immediately prior to any software installation or maintenance. It must be remembered that UNIX is a multi-user operating system and, as such, the responsibility for the maintenance of the filing system should be the responsibility of all who use it. The systems administrator should not interfere with user accounts unless a problem is encountered. Instead, the users should be made responsible for the maintenance of their own filing system. This means the users must be trained in the maintenance of filing systems and they must be encouraged to undertake such maintenance. Systems administrators can set a disk quota for each user, that limits the storage space they have available. Setting a 'reasonable' quota is essential as it enforces maintenance discipline in the users and protects the system from large increases in stored data.

Managing systems: backup

Perhaps the single most important task in managing any computer system is providing for its continuity. This involves protecting the organisation's data – most organisations cannot survive without access to it, and the following five ways of protecting data are frequently recommended:

- backup;
- backup;
- backup;
- backup;
- backup.

This is not a misprint – it is intentional. Users and systems administrators must realise that the only way an organisation can retrieve lost data is if it was backed up in the first place. Without a backup there is little chance of an organisation being able to retrieve its data. When it can, this is often very expensive and takes a long time. Data is the lifeblood of an organisation and, if it is starved of its data, it is unlikely it will be able to survive uninjured. If the data loss were complete, the organisation would probably not survive. Consider a credit card company that lost all its customers' balances – it would probably never be able to recoup all money it was owed. If a bank had major problems and lost the balance of its customers' accounts, how would their customers react?

It should also be understood that most systems change on a frequent basis – especially the data. As such, regular backups should be taken and the organisation should be prepared to lose any data that isn't backed up. The organisation should ask itself how much data it is prepared to lose – if the answer is 'very little', regular backups must be taken. Backups cannot be undertaken piecemeal: they are essential to the well-being of the organisation. As such it should be made someone's responsibility, on his or her job description, to take regular backups, and someone else's responsibility to ensure they are taking place. If not, they may not happen, which could result in catastrophe. Backups must be planned and a set of 'idiot-proof' instructions produced to ensure everyone understands how to take a backup.

Backup now complete, what next?

It is no good simply backing up a computer and trusting the backup has worked. The backup needs to be tested to ensure the data has been copied. The tape's test needs to be thorough – a backup is only as good as its test. Occasionally, someone should take a tape listing from the backup tape to verify everything has been written. However, on most tapes the backup directory is at the very front of the tape and the directory may well have been written but nothing else. The only way a backup can be truly tested is to restore all the files.

Unless the organisation has a separate computer with the same version of the operating system installed, this is usually not possible and an alternative must be found. However, the files should never be restored on to the same computer – if the backup has failed the original files will be corrupted.

If the organisation does not have a 'spare' computer, it is best to write a script that places a copy of a master text file around the filing system in predetermined locations (usually around mission critical data – both before and after it). The backup should then be taken and these text files removed from the computer. An attempt should then be made to restore the files from the backup and compare them to the master. If the copies verify OK, there is a high probability the backup will be OK. If not, another backup should be made immediately on another tape.

Backups can be made easily on UNIX using either the **tar** or **cpio** commands. The **tar** command normally has the following syntax:

> tar –cvf /dev/rmt0   for backup
> tar –tvf /dev/rmt0   for tape listing
> tar –xvf /dev/rmt0   for the extraction of files.

Figure 10.3 shows **tar** being used to create a backup, to list the contents of the backup and, finally, to restore two files.

> $
> $ tar -cvf backdir/up/bup date*.*
> a date.txt 1K
> a date2.txt 1K
> $
> $ tar -tvf backdir/bup
> tar: blocksize=6
> -rw-r-r-1069/10   34 Apr 26 11:34 1999 date.txt
> -rw------1069/10   34 Apr 26 11:341999 date2.txt
> $rm da*.*
> $is–l da*.*
> da*.*:No such file or directory
> $tar =xvf backdir/bup date.txt
> ta: blocksize=6
> x date.txt, 34 bytes, 1 tape blocks
> $ tar -xvf backdir/bup date 2.txt
> tar: blocksize=6
> x date2.txt, 34 bytes, 1 tape blocks
> $

Figure 10.3: Sample tar output

Further details can be obtained from the manual entries of **tar**. Users should be wary that **tar** could corrupt certain types of files (only the backup copy is corrupt). These include ORACLE databases, which must either be exported (an ORACLE command) prior to backup or must be backed up using **cpio** (which does not corrupt).

KEY CONCEPT

Backups must be tested regularly to prove the data can be restored.

Types of backup

There are three main backup techniques, and the selection of the most appropriate technique is just as important as selecting the right backup device.

Full

Performing a full backup on a frequent basis is usually the best way of protecting the system. This involves taking a copy of all the data, applications and systems files (including the operating system) and storing these to tape. Everything on the system is copied to tape, which requires a backup device with a large storage capacity. Because of the volume of information being stored, this type of backup takes the longest to perform. Should the organisation need 24-hour access to its data, this kind of backup can be disruptive. However, because all the information is on one backup set, this type of backup is the quickest way of restoring the system.

Full backups are perhaps easiest in UNIX and can be achieved simply by using the standard **tar** command: **tar –cvf /dev/rmt0**.

Incremental

Incremental backups are used to cut down the time taken for a full backup. Using this method, a full backup is taken and then the first incremental backup copies only the files modified (be they system or data files) since the full backup. The second incremental backup copies only those files (system or data) modified since the first incremental backup, and so on. This drastically cuts down on the time taken to back up, but can lead to a complex chain of tapes as each tape contains only files modified since the last backup. This means it would take a lot longer to restore the files and that the backup is dependent upon more tapes, which increases the probability of failure.

To make an incremental backup in UNIX, we need to 'find' the appropriate files and use this list to perform the backup. The find command in UNIX finds all the files that have been modified today: find / -mtime –1 ! –type d –print. This command will find all files starting from the root directory (/). The ! means not and the **–type d** means directory. Thus it will not find directories, as not everything in the directory will have changed.

UNIX permits command substitution, which allows a user to use a command in place of a string or a variable. This is achieved using the ' quotes, usually located at the top left of the keyboard. Thus the above command can be incorporated into the **tar** command: **tar -cvf / dev/rmt0 ' find / -mtime -1 ! -type d -print'**, giving a list of modified files to be backed up.

Differential

Differential backup is really a compromise between the previous two backup techniques. With differential backup, a full backup is taken and then subsequent differential backups. Each differential backup copies all files modified since the **last full backup**. This affords a higher level of protection than incremental backups, but not as high as a full backup. It also takes longer to back up than an incremental backup, but less time than a full backup. Finally, it takes longer to restore than a full backup but not as long as an incremental backup.

Differential backups in UNIX require a slightly different version of the find command. When the full backup is taken, the systems administrator creates a file (e.g. **/tmp/lastbackup**) that would have the date and time of the backup contained within it. The above command could then be modified to search for files that are newer than this: **tar -cvf /dev/rmt0 ' find . -newer /tmp/lastbackup ! –type d -print'**. Thus all the files that have been modified since the date of the **/tmp/lastbackup** file will be archived. The date and time of the **/tmp/lastbackup** file can be easily modified using the touch command: touch **/tmp/lastbackup**.

> ### KEY CONCEPT
>
> The time taken to restore is of the utmost importance – this is the time when you need the greatest speed. Fast backups are also important – normal business should not be interfered with. Therefore full backups are always recommended unless there are compelling reasons not to do so.

Backup cycles

Introduction

Tapes must be used in accordance with the manufacturer's guidelines (in terms of heat, humidity and acclimatisation) and should also be cycled. The manufacturers issue instructions with tapes detailing constraints on their use, which must be adhered to. The cycling of tapes is of the utmost importance – each tape should be used frequently and to a similar extent. Tapes stretch as they are used, especially at first. If they are underused, reliability may be impaired just as if they are overused. Systems administrators should ensure each tape is used a similar number of times. This cannot be achieved by random selection. Therefore two cycling techniques are discussed below that allow for the efficient cycling of tapes (the second affords a high level of protection, assuming a full backup is taken every night).

Grandfather/father/son

This is perhaps one of the simplest yet most effective backup cycles. The first tape created becomes the son and is kept. The second tape created becomes the new son, the older one becoming the father. When the third tape is used, this becomes the son, the oldest tape becomes the grandfather and the previous son becomes the father.

Thus there is a whole generation of backup tapes and it is possible to recover back to the third backup. In a daily cycle, this means that files lost up to three days ago can be recovered. As computer systems become larger with more users, lost files are often not noticed in three days. For example, consider a part-time class at a university – they may only be in university once a week. If they discover a lost file, it is too late to recover it using this method of cycling. Thus organisations have adopted more complex strategies for cycling. +

Four-week cycle

This method preserves each week's backups for a further four weeks. Full backups are taken on separate tape sets every business day. The last working day's tape is kept and the remainder are reused. This pattern is repeated for week two to week four. In week five, the first weekly backup tape is brought back into service. Assuming all data can be fitted on to one cartridge and assuming five working days, this requires 24 cartridges. However, the weekly tapes should not be used solely for weekly backups – this would underuse them and so they could fail.

> ### TIPS & ADVICE
>
> Backups should be kept for a 'reasonable' time. The definition of reasonable will depend upon the organisation.

Additional considerations

The following should also be considered when undertaking backups:

- Replace tapes regularly (the purchase date should be written on the tape, together with a tally of the number of times used).
- Upon receiving any errors, the tape should be replaced immediately.

- Clean the drive regularly, following the manufacturer's instructions.
- Always store tapes offsite in a fireproof safe.

Quick test

Discuss the major management issues a systems administrator should attend to.

Section 3: Disaster recovery planning

Introduction

Almost all organisations are critically dependent upon access to their data and are usually unable to function without access to it. For such organisations, the use of IT systems for data storage can be both a lifeline and a threat. Consider a credit card company whose premises have burnt to the ground. With copies of their data stored off site and access to a similar IT system, the company would be able to operate as normal within a very short space of time. However, if the reverse were true – the company had access to its premises but had lost access to its data, they would be highly unlikely to survive.

Almost all organisations will have insurance policies and hardware maintenance contracts, but what neither usually provide is a solution from the equipment being lost until the replacement arrives or repair is undertaken – that is the role of Disaster Recovery Planning.

Backups

Disaster recovery planning is crucially dependent upon backups – if you don't have up-to-date backups, then there will be nothing to restore on the replacement computers or in the alternate premises. You must make sure that:

1. you have current backups;
2. they are stored securely off-site, preferably in a fireproof safe;
3. the backups have been thoroughly tested;
4. software disks/licences are also stored securely off site.

Disasters

Disasters in this context means anything that prevents the organisation from being able to access its data and can include security breaches, Denial of Service (DoS) attacks as well as the usual fire, theft and flood. *Figure 10.4* summarises the leading causes of data loss.

Hardware or System Malfunction	44%
Human Error	32%
Software Corruption or Program Malfunction	14%
Computer Viruses	7%
Natural Disasters	3%

**Figure 10.4: Leading causes of data loss
(source: Ontrack Data Recovery)**

You cannot prevent disasters from happening, but you can carry out risk assessment, minimise the risks and adequately plan for disaster recovery.

Risk assessment

Risk assessment is the process of identifying risks that your organisation faces. There are generally two methods of risk assessment, which are complimentary:

1. An objective survey of the organisation to identify any risks.

2. A brainstorming session with key individuals.

When carrying out risk assessment it is important to identify as many risks as you can, encourage 'thinking outside the box' when brainstorming. Don't forget to think of internal risks as well as external – most computer fraud (around 2/3) is committed by employees. Once the risks have been identified, they need to be prioritised. This is known as exposure and is obtained by multiplying the value of a risk by its likelihood of occurrence. By minimising the risk you reduce your exposure. *Figure 10.5* shows an example of risk assessment.

Example of risk assessment/minimisation

You have an expensive mountain bike and decide to leave it unlocked in a particularly nasty neighbourhood, where it is almost certain to be stolen. The bike is worth £1,000 and you are 99% (.99 probability) certain it will be stolen. Your exposure is £1,000 x .99 = £990. Suppose you add a very expensive lock that will protect the whole bike, you estimate that this will reduce the risk of theft to 50% (.5 probability). You have reduced your exposure to £500. By not leaving the bike in that neighbourhood and using the lock you reduce the chance of theft to 10% (.1 probability). Your exposure is now £100. You could of course insure your bike and pass on the risk, but what would you do in between your bike being stolen and it being replaced?

Figure 10.5: An example of risk assessment

Planning

Disaster recovery planning is about planning for business continuity in the event of a disaster and hoping it never happens. Most auditors now like to see that the organisation has thought about disaster recovery planning and will often ask to see your disaster recovery plan.

The essence of disaster recovery planning is to identify whether disasters will:

● stop you using your premises;

● stop you accessing your data; or

● stop you using your hardware.

For example, the car bomb that struck Commercial Union London in 1992 blew out all of the windows in their tower block. This rendered the building unusable but, because they had multiple data links, they were still able to access data remotely and, using a register of unused space in branch offices, were able to open for business as usual on Monday following the blast the previous Friday.

In order to effectively plan for disasters you need to identify what you would do in each of the situations. There are a number of options, which are briefly described below:

Self-protection

Large organisations with multiple premises may well be able to protect themselves. Consider a university with a number of different buildings spread across a city using PCs and UNIX machines. If disaster struck one of the key business units, for example finance, providing the data was in tact, the finance department could relocate into one of the other buildings, perhaps a teaching building. Assume it took over a PC lab and had the phones re-routed. Providing the department had made arrangements to take over a UNIX machine and the lab in times of disaster, it could move into the classroom, load the data, organise the telephones and be 'open for business' relatively quickly. Disruption to classes could be handled either by using spare capacity in other labs, or at worst, altering the working hours of finance to work when the class was empty.

Smaller organisations may well be able to achieve this too – a small accountancy or law practice may be able to easily work out of a home.

In the case of network self-protection, you may wish to keep spare kit or spread connections so that if, say, a switch fails, you can move all of the connections to spare capacity on other switches. Some spare wireless kit could prove very useful in recovering from a network disaster.

KEY CONCEPT

Whilst self-protection seems relatively straightforward, you must plan for it. You must also make sure that you have the expertise available to make it possible – if your support team isn't available, how will you make the move?

Mutual protection

Mutual protection is where two or more organisations enter into an agreement to offer space and services to each other should disaster strike. These types of plans tend to be more suitable for organisations that aren't in competition with each other, for example schools and colleges – if School A is unable to access its administrative data, it could move to School B with its data and carry out its business.

If you think this type of plan may be suitable, you should carefully draft a legal agreement. All parties should also monitor relevant changes with the other parties, for example changes of equipment, available space, changes of management, etc. Overall, the parties should ask themselves: 'Am I prepared to stake my organisation on this?'.

Commercial plans

There are a number of companies who offer commercial plans for disaster recovery. These plans range from sending your data to the company who will load it onto their machine and provide you with remote access, up to a 'white room' service. A white room is an unused room complete with all computer equipment, desks, chairs, telephones – everything an organisation would need to carry on business should disaster strike. Some companies have mobile offices that can be towed by truck and set up in the casualty organisation's car park.

Obviously, the price varies according to the service you want. In between, companies are likely to offer you a loan of a machine (for a specified time) or perhaps even send a technical team to help you get up and running again.

Factors that should be considered when entering in to a commercial agreement are:

- Types of computers the company use – are they compatible with your own and will you be able to simply use them without any specialist training?

- The ratio of computers kept to the number of clients the company has – a company keeping 1 computer for every 10 clients is likely to be a safer option than a company keeping 1 computer for every 100 clients.

- Ability to upgrade the plan in times of disaster – if disaster strikes and your technical team aren't available will you be able to upgrade to get the contractors technical team?

- The length of the loan of equipment – will it be long enough for you to process the insurance claim and to cover the lead times with your kit?

- The expertise available in the company – will it meet your needs?

- Testimonials from those who have suffered disaster and used the companies service.

- Financial stability of the company.

- Lead time before the company will have you back up and running.

- Clauses allowing you to test their services.

Testing your disaster recovery plan

Auditors may be happy that you have a disaster recovery plan in place, but will it actually work if disaster strikes? Having gone so far down the line most organisations are now worried and want assurances that it will work. The only way to convince yourself of this is to simulate a disaster and try out your plan. For example, pretend that your system has gone down or that disaster has struck and try moving to your white room and recover the operation. Most disaster recovery companies will allow you to test out their services, but there will obviously be a charge for this.

TIPS & ADVICE

Never try simulating a disaster by deleting data from your system – if your plans don't work, you may well have a real disaster on your hands!

KEY CONCEPT

All disaster recovery plans are critically dependent upon planning, backups and keeping the plans up-to-date. Make sure that you plan everything:

- Keeping an up to date telephone directory (copy off site!), which includes a means of contacting your key members of staff wherever they are.
- Taking regular backups and keeping them off-site.
- Monitoring your disaster recovery plans and keeping them in contract and up to date.
- Monitoring the health of your disaster recovery provider.
- Regularly testing your backups.
- Testing your disaster recovery plans.

TIPS & ADVICE

Remember we all have a part to play in this – if the organisation goes down, we will lose our jobs and perhaps our lifestyle.

Quick Test

Briefly name and discuss the various types of disaster recovery plans available.

Virus protection

Computer viruses are yet another threat to networks and systems. Unfortunately, the development of networks and emails means they can be spread more quickly than they could by floppy disks. The security policy must deal with the threat of computer viruses, which can lead either to a denial of service or can be used to open a 'back door' into the system. With viruses, prevention is definitely better than cure. Protecting the system from viruses involves educating the end-users in the need to be aware of the risks of computer viruses and how they are spread, etc. The organisation's policy must aim to minimise the threat of viruses, and the users must work to this policy, either by choice or by force – but the former is more acceptable! Such a policy must:

- regulate the use of floppy disks and CD-ROMs in the organisation;
- control the sending and receiving of email attachments;
- control downloads from the web;
- control the installation of software;
- ensure that every machine has an up-to-date virus checker installed;
- ensure that each machine is regularly updated with the latest version of the antivirus software.

Users should be discouraged from using CD-ROMs or floppy disks unless they can demonstrate a need and they have been virus checked. Some organisations make unauthorised use a disciplinary offence. Sending and, particularly, receiving email attachments should be discouraged unless absolutely necessary. Even when necessary, these attachments should be in a zipped form rather than executable. This facilitates easier virus checking on the receiving machine. Remember, plain ASCII text is always safe – it is the attachments, etc., that cause the problems. Downloads from the web are extremely dangerous and users should be discouraged from downloading (and certainly installing) software and files. Indeed, the only software that can be safely installed is shrink-wrapped software from a trusted manufacturer or supplier. Each machine should have a reputable, up-to-date virus checker installed, and this must be kept up to date with the latest releases from the manufacturer.

The network operating system also needs to be chosen carefully. A system that offers a high degree of security (with separate logins for each user) and administration rights to the administrator only, will go a long way to protecting itself. Should a virus somehow sneak in to the system, under such conditions it should not be able to infect easily either other users' files or the operating system itself. Regular system backups must be taken and several generations should be kept – restoring yesterday's infected file is of little use, but last week's out-of-date uninfected file is of use. These backups should be on external media that can be removed from the system and stored safely. Again, the anti-virus policy must be continuously monitored and updated if it is to remain effective.

KEY CONCEPT

Viruses are a real threat to organisations. Good administration is essential to minimise this threat.

Quick test

Briefly outline the major items that should be covered in an organisation's security and anti-virus policy.

Section 4: End of chapter assessment

Questions

1. Discuss the major steps involved in creating users and groups in the UNIX operating system. You should pay particular attention to such issues as policy.

2. Briefly discuss the major tasks involved in managing a network and the importance of these tasks.

3. Briefly discuss the process of risk assessment and disaster recovery planning, stating why it is a necessary practice for most organisations.

Answers

1. This question is in two parts. The first asks you to discuss the major steps involved in creating users and groups on a UNIX system. The second is interested in the control of that creation. For the first part, you need to discuss how an account is created on a UNIX system, outlining the various steps needed to create the account, the group and to allocate the user to a group. For the second part, you should discuss the possible security implications of creating a user or a group and adding/deleting users from that group. Your answer should ideally mention the fact that a user ID is the key to accessing the system and that unauthorised accounts could compromise systems security. You should discuss the need for (and outline), an administrative process that would create accounts/ groups and allocate users to those groups in a secure manner.

2. To answer this question, you need to identify the major tasks involved in managing a network. For each task, you need to discuss briefly the task and its importance in aiding the smooth operation of the network. In the case of more specific tasks, such as backups, you should briefly discuss the various options available and, if possible, outline any advice you would give concerning the best methods to back up systems and data.

3. To answer this question, you identify the stages of disaster recovery planning: risk assessment, planning, and the variety of disaster recovery options available. Ideally, you should discuss briefly discuss each option and identify the advantages and disadvantages. A good idea would be to remind the assessor of the need to keep regular backups and to test them – it shows a greater understanding of the problem.

Section 5: Further reading and research

Afzal, A. (2002) *UNIX Unbounded: A Beginning Approach*. Prentice Hall. ISBN 0 13092 736 8.

Cisco Networking Academy Program (2004) *CCNA 1 and 2 Companion Guide*, (3rd edn). Cisco Press. ISBN: 1 58713 150 1. Chapters 8 and 28.

For main commands in Unix, see **www.fedora.redhat.com**

Chapter 11
Connecting to the outside world

Chapter summary

This chapter provides an overview of networking by illustrating how all the equipment works together in order to provide connectivity. Since the Internet is a hot topic at the moment, it outlines how a request for a web page is generated on a PC and handled by the network.

Learning outcomes

After studying this chapter you should aim to test your achievement of the following outcomes. You should be able to:

Outcome 1: Types of Internet connections
Understand the differences between the main types of Internet connections and be able to select the most appropriate for a particular situation. Question 1 at the end of this chapter will test you on this.

Outcome 2: The Internet (TCP/IP) case study
Understand how the Internet operates when requesting and receiving web pages. Question 2 at the end of this chapter will test you on this.

How will you be assessed on this?

Knowing how connection to the Internet and how data travels in the form packets and frames (crossing internal networks and the Internet) will give you the 'big picture' of how networks operate. Even if this is not assessed directly, it will deepen your understanding, which will come through in any assessment you undertake. In a practical assessment, you could be asked to recommend an Internet connection for a given company. You could also be asked in an exam to discuss how connection to the Internet can be achieved and how data is exchanged. You can, of course, weave the content of this chapter into most of your answers for extra marks.

Section 1: Types of Internet connections

Currently there are only two possible ways to connect to the Internet: dial-up lines and local area networks. For the purposes of this chapter, ADSL and cable are considered to be LAN connections, although the chapter does explain briefly how ADSL and cable work.

Dial-up connection

Most people are familiar with this method of connecting to the Internet and it is still by far the most popular, with more than 50% of users still connecting in this fashion. Dial-up connection involves the use of a pair of modems and a telephone line. The modems convert the digital computer signals into analogue signals that are suitable for transmission over the telephone network. Another modem at the other end converts them back. This is known as a point-to-point (PPP) serial link and is available through virtually all ISPs. Once at the ISP's premises, the data is transferred on to its LAN and begins its journey to the Internet. Dial-up connection is also known as plain old telephone service or POTS for short. Typically, modems provide 33.6 K upload speed and 56.6 K download speed.

ADSL

Asymmetric digital subscriber line (ASDL) is a method by which a permanent connection to the Internet can be provided to an end-subscriber using existing telephone lines. Quite simply, this is achieved by dividing the bandwidth of the conventional telephone line into channels, in a similar way that the bandwidth of TV/radio broadcasts is divided into channels (BBC1, BBC2, ITV1, etc.) (see Figure 11.1). Technically, this is known as Frequency Division Multiplexing (FDM). Frequency ranges are allocated to particular services. In the case of ADSL, a small frequency range is allocated to the telephone service, a second, larger frequency range to the upstream connection to the Internet and the third, and largest channel to the downstream link to the Internet. Connection requires a device to split the channels (often called a **microfilter**) and a broadband modem. The computer and telephone can then attach to the microfilter.

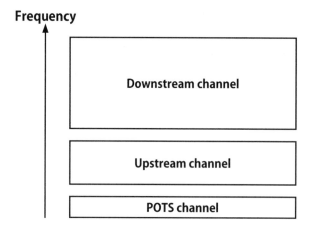

Figure 11.1: ADSL channels

Although the theory sounds straightforward, the cable and equipment that carry ADSL were never meant for this purpose, and so the technology that makes this possible is nothing short of a miracle!

'Asymmetric' means the line is imbalanced in favour of receiving data – with ADSL it is possible to receive at more than 2 Mbps, but outbound transmission is limited to around 128 Kbps. As most home connections surf the web and download files, video and music, ADSL is ideally suited for this purpose. However, if a web server was connected or an organisation made large and frequent transmissions, ADSL would not be so suitable. There would be a considerable difference in speed when downloading a file compared to uploading.

DSL technology has been a godsend to the telephone companies. It has allowed them to provide high bandwidth data rates to dispersed locations with relatively small changes to the existing telephone infrastructure. DSL technologies seem likely to develop in the coming decade, delivering an even higher bandwidth.

The two main disadvantages to ADSL are that it is only available up to 5.5 km from the telephone exchange and not all exchanges are kitted out to support it. Range may increase as technology develops.

Cable modems

Many parts of the country have now been provided with Internet access through cable TV systems. In most parts of the UK, the cable systems that have been installed have been designed to transfer data, and it is common to find integrated cable modems inside cable TV boxes. Again, using Frequency Division Multiplexing (FDM), data is effectively added to the cable system using a separate, dedicated frequency. However, because the cable is under the control of the cable company and has a much greater bandwidth than twisted pair, cable companies are able to tailor their service and to offer higher data rates than ADSL. For example, most cable companies can offer at least a 4 Mbps connection and they can tailor its direction – a residential customer is more likely to download information than to upload and so the cable company will provide a faster downstream connection than upstream. A web-hosting company would probably want the connection the other way around.

Like DSL, cable modems provide a permanent connection to the Internet: they are always on, and when the computer is on, they can represent a security hazard. Usually, the frequency used by the cable companies is employed to provide an extended Ethernet network over a WAN, with a geographical reach of up to 100 miles. It is therefore not unusual to see a cable box with a dedicated Ethernet port at the rear.

ISDN

Integrated Services Digital Network (ISDN) was and still is very popular in the USA but never really caught on in the UK, largely due to price. With ISDN, a telephone subscriber is provided with two digital telephone lines. If they are used for voice, they require special telephones to be connected to them. The most common ISDN connection is ISDN2, which provides two bearer (or B) channels each of which can carry 64 Kbps and one Delta (or D) channel that establishes and manages the session. Thus ISDN provides a maximum of 128 Kbps in either direction. This must, of course, be matched by the ISP. The subscriber pays call costs for ISDN and also for the line rental for each of the lines. Thus a one-hour Internet session will cost twice as much as a one hour phone call and along with the rental for the two lines, this makes it very expensive when compared to ADSL.

ISDN is now mainly used for video conferencing and for large organisations that require an infrequently used backup line for WAN connections. ISDN is usually available as ISDN2, ISDN6 and ISDN30. The number represents the number of lines and hence the bearer channels. Thus for ISDN30 there are 30 lines, thirty 64 Kbps channels, 30 line rental charges to pay and 30 times the call-costs. ISDN in the USA and Japan is slightly different from that in the UK and most of Europe.

Satellite

Since 2003, companies began offering broadband connection speeds through a combination of satellite and telephone technology (*Figure 11.2*). Although this method has been available for some time, it is the use of the Sky Digital satellite system that makes this an affordable option – previously it was via a dedicated satellite.

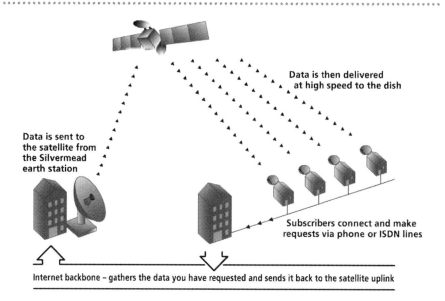

Data is sent to the satellite from the Silvermead earth station

Data is then delivered at high speed to the dish

Subscribers connect and make requests via phone or ISDN lines

Internet backbone – gathers the data you have requested and sends it back to the satellite uplink

Figure 11.2 Broadband via satellite (courtesy of Silvermead)

This type of technology is probably most suitable for those who can't receive broadband services because of their location – remember, ADSL requires technology to be added to telephone exchanges, which could take quite some time in rural areas. Also, some subscribers are too far from their exchange to have ADSL. As shown in *Figure 11.2*, this technology uses the existing telephone line to send a request, say, for a web page to the ISP. The ISP then retrieves the page from the Internet at high speed and returns it via the satellite to the user. This should happen as quickly as conventional broadband services. The technology requires a satellite modem and a modification to a conventional satellite receiver. The main disadvantage of this technology is that it ties up a conventional telephone line. Other than that, as a service it is virtually identical to broadband – around 33 Kbps outbound and around 0.5 Mbps inbound.

Private wire

Organisations such as web-hosting companies, large institutions, e-commerce sites and universities that require very high-speed connection to the Internet can connect using private wires. These are private dedicated connections from the organisation to its ISP usually using fibre optic cabling. Using technologies such as ATM (*see Chapter 5*), this link can be as high as 1 Gbps (providing the receiving ISP can handle it) but it is very expensive.

Mobile connections

Mobile connections provide a means of connecting to the Internet using the mobile phone network. Although this has been possible for a number of years, the connection speeds were slow (around 9.6 Kbps). Third generation (3G) mobile networks are changing that providing a connection speed of up to 384 Kbps inbound (almost 7 times faster than standard dial up – remember early broadband was 128 Kbps) and 64 Kbps outbound using a 3G data card (*Figure 11.3*).

**Figure 11.3: A 3G data card
(connects into a laptop using PCMCIA slot)**

If 3G is not available, the cards will usually default to General Packet Radio Service (GPRS), which provides a modem speed 56 Kbps connection.

3G is making truly mobile data possible. If the costs are appealing and coverage can be widened, 3G data is sure to grow.

TIPS & ADVICE

It is important you understand the various connections to the Internet and their characteristics. You will almost certainly be asked about this in an assessment.

KEY CONCEPT

Different types of Internet connection have different attributes. When deciding on a connection, the one that best matches the client's requirements should be chosen. Of course, it is important to make sure their ISP can handle it.

Quick test

Briefly discuss the major ways of connecting to the Internet.

Section 2: The Internet (TCP/IP) case study

Throughout this book, standards, equipment, topologies and technologies have been discussed. Whilst understanding all this is of crucial importance, we still have not considered the 'big picture' – i.e. how does it all work? If, for example, an Ethernet or cable modem was chosen, how would the web browser download the information from the Internet? How does it find the information?

This section intends to answer these questions by outlining the process of connecting to the Internet and retrieving a web page. This section assumes an Ethernet network connection is being used. If a modem is being used, a serial link is simply being employed that connects to the ISP's LAN – it looks exactly the same except the connection to the PC from the LAN is serial.

Your Internet settings

Every computer connected to the Internet needs a minimum of three settings: an IP address, a subnet mask and a default gateway. These can be obtained either by going into the network settings from the control panel or by running the **winipcfg** command (Windows 98) or the ipconfig command (Windows NT, 2000 and XP). *Figure 11.4* shows sample output from the **winipcfg** command. If set to automatic, the computer will obtain its IP address form a DHCP (Dynamic Host Configuration Protocol) server.

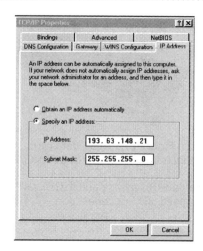

**Figure 11.4: Ethernet settings
(networking option from control panel in Windows 98)**

Looking at each of the settings in turn, the adaptor address is the MAC address of the Ethernet NIC (*see Chapter 5*). The IP address is the computer's logical address on the Internet (*see Chapter 3*) and the subnet mask is a binary pattern used to locate the network. The default gateway is the place to which the computer sends the packet if it has no idea what else to do with it.

In the IP address, the first byte tells us that this is a class C address (because it is in the class C address range – *see Chapter 3*). Thus the first three bytes are used to specify the network address (in this case 193.63.148). The subnet mask (*see Chapter 3*) 255.255.255.0 tells us to compare the first three bytes to determine the subnetwork. Thus we can see that the default gateway is on the same subnetwork as the machine itself (because the first three bytes are identical). An address of 18.98.38.1 would be on a different subnet.

However, how does this relate to a web page? A URL is essentially a text representation of an IP address. When we enter a URL (e.g. **osiris.sunderland.ac.uk**) into a web browser, the web browser communicates with a domain name server (DNS) and retrieves the IP address but it doesn't display it. So if 157.228.102.1 is keyed into your browser, it will retrieve the same page as if **osiris.sunderland.ac.uk** had been keyed in. To locate the DNS server, the machine broadcasts an Ethernet frame asking the DNS server to make itself known.

TIPS & ADVICE

Examine the settings on your PC and then try keying 157.228.102.1 into your browser.

Beginning the journey

Figure 11.5 represents an Internet connection.

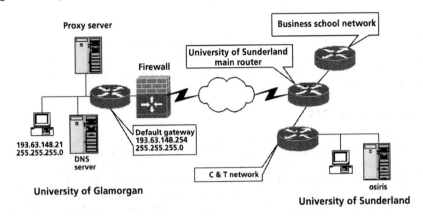

Figure 11.5: An Internet connection

A PC at the University of Glamorgan is being used to view the home page of the School of Computing and Technology at the University of Sunderland (**osiris.sunderland.ac.uk**). Both networks are Ethernet. The URL is entered into the browser, which immediately queries the DNS server and retrieves the IP address of 157.228.102.1. It does this by broadcasting an Ethernet frame to the DNS server which then responds with a unicast frame (to one machine only) containing the IP address. For our purposes it does not matter how the DNS server knows the address – very crudely, all DNSs across the world talk to one another to update their tables.

The machine at Glamorgan now knows the address of **osiris.sunderland.ac.uk** as 157.228.102.1. It uses its subnet mask to identify the parts of the address that give the network address (*see Chapter 3*). It does this by logic: by ANDing the address and the subnet mask together. In binary 255 is 11111111 – all bits are 1 in the byte. A bit set to 1 means compare. Thus 255.255.255.0 means compare all parts of the first three bytes. The network portion of the IP address is therefore 193.63.148 (the last byte is the host ID – the Glamorgan PC in this case). As 193.63.148 and 157.228.102 are not identical, the PC knows the machine it is looking for is not on the same network as itself.

> **KEY CONCEPT**
>
> This very brief description of subnetworking (or subnetting) is fundamental to networking and the Internet. Networks are divided to lessen the load on them. In *Chapter 6* we saw that a bridge or switch can help control collisions but they can't control broadcasts – routers and subnets are needed for this. More information on subnetting is contained in *Chapter 3*.

The Glamorgan machine does not know what to do with the packet. However, it has been programmed to send such packets to the default gateway. Although the PC knows the IP address of the default gateway, it has no idea of the MAC address of the default gateway. To find the MAC address, it needs to resolve the IP address. It does this through a process known as Address Resolution Protocol (ARP). The machine broadcasts an Ethernet frame which asks the machine that has the IP address of 193.63.148.254 to respond with its MAC address. The default gateway router receives this broadcast and realises the IP address is its own. It then responds with a unicast frame to the Glamorgan PC. It can unicast because it knows the Glamorgan PC's MAC address – it was in its frame – and, obviously, it knows its own address. Unicasts are preferable to broadcasts as they do not consume as much network bandwidth (they go to one machine only, not all the machines).

The Glamorgan PC now knows the MAC address of the default gateway, and it encapsulates the IP packet requesting the web page into an Ethernet frame addressed to the default gateway. This frame is placed on to the Ethernet network where it begins its journey to the default gateway.

The proxy server

In the event the University of Glamorgan uses a proxy server, the browser will itself request that the IP address of the requested web page is sent to the proxy. It does this for two reasons. The first is to establish if the proxy already holds a copy of that web page. It if does, it can retrieve it more quickly and less expensively than if it went to the Internet (ISPs and directly connected companies are charged for the use of certain links, e.g. Transatlantic). Secondly, it checks the organisation's security policy – is this URL allowed? The proxy server then handles the retrieval of the web page itself, sending it to the default gateway.

The default gateway

If the proxy server and/or the PC don't know the whereabouts of a web page, the request lands at the default gateway. The default gateway is usually a router and it may have a number of routes connected to it. As we saw in *Chapter 6*, routers have two purposes – to determine the best path and to switch the packet. In this case, the router needs to determine which of the paths it is directly connected to will lead to the required IP address. It isn't feasible for a router to know every IP address on the Internet and so it, too, has a default gateway: if it doesn't know what to do with a packet it forwards it to its default gateway.

In our example, the University of Glamorgan router is connected only to the Internet and the Glamorgan network. As a 157.228.102 address clearly doesn't belong to the University of Glamorgan, the router has no idea what to do with it and so sends it to its default gateway – in this case, on to the Internet.

Firewall

Before passing on to the Internet, the packet may be subjected to a firewall. A firewall is a piece of software whose purpose is to provide greater network security. A firewall can be thought of as a collection of numbered, and guarded exit doors to an organisation: employees have to leave by certain numbered doors and, if the doors are locked (perhaps it's not time for them to leave), they can't get out. If the door is unlocked, they can leave but they may be subjected to a search to determine if they are carrying any secrets.

A firewall does exactly the same thing with data. Data exiting from an organisation does so via port numbers (the door numbers in the analogy), which can be open or closed.

Commonly used port numbers are:

Port	Application
21	FTP
23	Telnet
25	SMTP
80	Web.

Packets passing through the firewall may also be subjected to a search to see if they contain any data that isn't allowed under the organisation's security policy. If they do, they are dealt with severely – they are destroyed!

> **KEY CONCEPT**
>
> Firewalls are an important part of an organisation's security, but they do not meet all an organisation's needs – they should be part of a policy that includes routers and proxy servers. The policy should also recognise network users. Without such an integrated policy, firewalls are of little use.

On to the Internet

If packets pass successfully through the firewall, they are ready to be placed on to the Internet. Almost certainly, the bandwidth of the organisation's Internet connection will be smaller than that of its LAN. Not all packets will be able to fit on to such a limited bandwidth and so some will be lost. TCP (transmission control protocol – *see Chapter 4*) waits for an acknowledgement from the recipient of the packets transmitted. In the event it does not receive one, it simply sends a replacement packet. Once on the Internet, the packets head toward huge routers with huge routing tables. When they arrive at these routers, their destination IP address is examined and, if the router knows the route the packet should take, it is switched to that route. If not, it is forwarded to that router's default gateway.

Often represented as a cloud (as in *Figure 11.5*), the Internet is a complex web of connections and routers. However, one thing that should be noted about the Internet is that it operates on TCP that is inherently reliable. As the Internet is such a mass of connections, each has several backups. For example, there are satellite connections between the UK and the USA, but there are also trans-oceanic cables and satellite connections to and from Europe to the USA. Thus a transmission will almost always get through even if links are down – the Internet will route around the downed links. The reliability of the Internet was harrowingly demonstrated on 11 September 2001. After the aircraft hit the World Trade Center, all conventional telephone services were lost. However, IP telephones were able to route around the downed links.

Arriving at the destination

Eventually the packet will approach the University of Sunderland and will arrive at its router. When it arrives, it will be immediately subjected to a firewall. If it is bound for an open door, it will be allowed. If not, it will simply be destroyed. Once through the door, it will be inspected by the firewall to determine if it is the sort of packet that should be allowed through. Providing it is, it is passed on to the university LAN (encapsulated in an Ethernet frame). After the firewall, a router, will examine the network element of the IP address and forward the packet to the appropriate network. Once it arrives on the appropriate network, the router on that network will either know the MAC address of osiris or it will ARP to get it. Once it has the MAC address of osiris, it will forward the IP packet (inside an Ethernet frame) to osiris. Osiris will open the packet and examine the contents – a request for a web page. Osiris will then recycle the packet, replacing the destination address with the source address (i.e. putting the address of the Glamorgan machine as the destination and its own address as the source).

The return journey

If the contents of the web page are too large to fit into one packet, the server will replicate the packet structure. It will then fill the packet with the required contents and send the packet back: to the default gateway, to the university proxy server, through the firewall and on to the Internet. Once it arrives at the University of Glamorgan, it will be subjected to the firewall and will then on to the university LAN. It will pass on to the proxy server (inside an Ethernet frame because it's on a LAN), which will check its contents. If the proxy allows the packet through, it will take a copy of it so that further requests for that web page can be satisfied from it rather than having to go on to the Internet. It will then be passed to the router to be delivered to the machine.

As the router knows the MAC address of this machine, it encapsulates the packet inside a frame and sends it to the machine. The machine strips off the Ethernet and IP headers, extracts the data and displays it. All this happens in the 'blink of an eye'.

Summary

In this discussion of the Internet and of how networks (in this case the Ethernet) facilitate the movement of traffic to and from the Internet, only the most important networking device – the router – has been highlighted. Typically, however, Ethernet frames would pass through a host of Ethernet networking devices, including switches and hubs.

KEY CONCEPT

Packets containing web page requests travel far – across Ethernet networks and the Internet and through many, varied devices.

Quick test

Briefly outline how a request for a web page generates both Ethernet frames and IP packets and how these result in the web page being retrieved and displayed.

Section 3: End of chapter assessment

Questions

1. Identify the most common ways of connecting a home PC to the Internet. Briefly discuss each, highlighting their advantages and disadvantages.

2. Briefly outline how a request for a web page makes its way to the Internet.

Answers

1. To answer this question, you need to list the most popular connections from the home to the Internet (i.e. modem access, DSL, cable and ISDN). For each of these connections, you need to discuss the features of the connection type – for example, always on, the equipment needed for the connection and the advantages and disadvantages. For instance, ADSL is asymmetric, which makes it ideal for connecting from the home: it has a faster downstream connection than upstream; there are no call costs; and it is faster than a conventional (modem) connection. You should also discuss the disadvantages – for example, it has a slower upload speed than download and, although still faster than a modem connection, it may not be suitable for all teleworking.

2. As you couldn't possibly discuss all that is covered in this chapter in an exam question, this question is only concerned with how a request for a web page makes its way from the PC to the Internet. In practice, networks are most likely to be Ethernet, and so you should state this before you start. The best place to start is a discussion of the network settings on a PC and what they mean and do. From that you can expand your answer to discuss how the PC decides whether or not the web server is on the same network as the PC. Assuming it is, it will cut out most of the answer to the question and a good part of your marks! Therefore assume it isn't and show the role of the default gateway, default gateways set on the router, the proxy server and the firewall.

Section 4: Further reading and research

Cisco Networking Academy Program (2001) *First Year Companion Guide* (2nd edn). Cisco Press. ISBN: 1 58713 025 4. Chapter 30.

Dick, D. (2003) *PC Support Handbook*. Dumbreck Publishing. ISBN: 0 95417 111 X. Data communications chapter.

Chapter 12
Network security

Chapter summary

Information security is often as paramount for organisations as it is for the military. Companies have commercially-sensitive information as well as having obligations under legislation such as the Data Protection Act and the European Data Directive. Before the widespread use of computers, information security was provided by rugged filing cabinets, perhaps a security guard and usually a personnel screening system. The aim was simple – to limit access to sensitive information.

Before the widespread use of computers, it was relatively easy to spot someone stealing information – long periods spent at the photocopier and carrying large boxes of paper out of the building!

With the widespread use of computers it is much easier – by using a DAT cartridge it is possible to steal 72 GB of data on a cartridge small enough to fit into a shirt pocket. To put 72 GB in context – the entire *Encyclopaedia Britannica* is around 1 GB! With networking you don't even need physical access!

This chapter guides you through the basics of network security, identifying the tools available, likely sources and the need for a co-ordinated plan. You must remember that network security is a huge subject and only a basic guide can be given – if in doubt seek specialist help.

Learning outcomes

After studying this chapter you should aim to test your achievement of the following outcomes. You should be able to:

Outcome 1: Security
Understand the need for network and system security and be able to evaluate security, devise, implement and monitor security policies. Question 1 at the end of this chapter will test your ability to do this.

Outcome 2: Security technologies
Understand the security technologies available and their place in a secure system. Question 2 at the end of this chapter will test your ability to do this

How will you be assessed on this?

This chapter is mainly theory and it is highly unlikely that your academic institution will have the time or the skills to have you implement security. As such, it is likely to be assessed as theory, perhaps asking you to draft a security plan as part of an assignment or discuss security technologies in an exam.

Section 1: Security

To be effective security must be a planned and co-ordinated effort based upon risk assessment (*see Chapter 10*) with various tools and techniques being brought together in a co-ordinated fashion to help secure the organisation.

It is very important to realise that threats change on an almost daily basis and that you must constantly monitor your security policy and devices, make improvements and test those improvements to ensure the best possible protection.

Introduction

Network security is a major topic in computing and not without reason. Most organisations are critically dependent upon their information, of which, the only copy is almost certainly held on computer. Theft or fraud involving that information is serious but even more serious is the organisation being denied access to its own information. Known as a denial of service attack, this may be as simple as someone accessing their computer system and changing all of the passwords.

In the main, the threats to a computer system are:

- misuse of the computer system;
- attacks on the network;
- computer viruses;
- disaster;
- data loss;
- theft of hardware.

To be effective, security must be a policy-based approach. The policy can then be implemented using a variety of techniques such as manual procedures, limiting end-user access, firewalls, routers and leased communication lines. This section briefly explores the main issues of network security and provides suggestions on countering these.

The most important piece of advice that can be given to protect the organisation is, to take regular backups of the system, to try out these backups, ensuring they work, and to store the backup tapes off site in a fireproof safe. Whilst this will in no way help prevent attacks on the computer system, it will provide the organisation with a way to recover if anything should happen (*see Chapter 10*). In the case of the last three items on the list, if you don't have backups you will probably never recover and the chances of your organisation continuing (let alone continuing unharmed) are not in your favour.

Misuse of the computer system

In the main, the problem of computer security is hard to quantify – many organisations that have fallen victim prefer to cover up the problem, as public exposure will cause even more damage. Consider a bank losing £2 million through poor computer security – would you be happy banking with them?

Various surveys have indicated that as much as 2/3 of all computer misuse is actually committed by employees of the organisation. Common sources of misuse include creating (and paying) bogus employees, creating dummy purchase orders and paying invoices, etc. Little technical ingenuity but plenty of scope for fraud. Policies need to be in place which makes it more difficult for such activities to take place. Physical separation of duties make it more difficult. For example the same person shouldn't pay the invoices as created the purchase order, similarly before creating an employee on the payroll system, a request must be received from Personnel.

Employees need to be educated not to share their user IDs and passwords. Someone using your ID or password is effectively you to all audit trails on the system. Should some fraud take place, it is you that will be accused.

Employees exceeding their level of security is also a problem. Assuming passwords are not shared, then the best way to tackle this possibility is to configure the user interface. For example, if the user's duties are only paying invoices, then menu systems should be created (*see Chapter 9*) that only offers this option. In this way, it becomes very difficult for the user to exceed their level of authority.

Attacks on the network

Surveys by the Computer Security Institute (CSI) found that 70% of organisations said their network security defences had been breached. And that 60% of the incidents came from within the organisation. Again, the internal threat is greater than the external threat.

Four types of network threat can be identified:

- unstructured threats;
- structured threats;
- external threats;
- internal threats.

Unstructured threats are mainly from inexperienced individuals using tools they downloaded from the internet. Whilst they aren't that technically competent, they have some sort of intent or wouldn't be 'having a go'. The fact that they are is a problem.

Structured threats are from seasoned hackers who are competent and motivated. They have an understanding of networking and more sophisticated tools.

External threats are as you would expect – from outside the organisation securing access through dial up connections or the Internet.

Internal threats are when someone has authorised access to the network or physical access to the networking devices.

Physical security of devices and major cabling is paramount – if someone can physically access your devices, then they can probably defeat the passwords (most equipment provides for password recovery from physical access). Similarly, if they have access to major cabling, simply cutting it will cause a great deal of harm.

Types of attack

Network attacks can be broadly categorised into three:

- reconnaissance attacks;
- access attacks;
- denial of Service (DoS) attacks.

Reconnaissance attacks

Reconnaissance attacks are akin to a burglar checking out a neighbourhood – looking for unlocked doors, half open windows, etc. They don't intend to carry out a burglary immediately, but are looking for weaknesses. Networks have similar weaknesses – they are looking for folders you may have made sharable in windows and forgotten to close, exposed UNIX directories, etc. Hackers will make a note of these weaknesses and come back to exploit them when fewer people are looking.

Access attacks

Access is a broad term referring to unauthorised data manipulation, systems access or privilege escalation. Data manipulation is viewing information that the intruder wasn't meant to have access to (this could include copying or moving the information). In order to carry this out, the intruder needs to gain access and, quite often, seasoned hackers will use tools to achieve access. In the same way as a burglar uses lock picks, hackers use either password crackers or other utilities, which either exploit a weakness in the system, or simply brute force (tirade of passwords) to gain access.

Access attacks that involve privilege escalation are ones in which legitimate users (or hackers who have succeeded in getting low-level access to the system) attempt to gain higher-level access. This can involve running some kind of software – perhaps a password-sniffing tool to identify passwords being sent across the network. Shared machines at universities and colleges are particularly prone to this kind of attack, so beware!

Denial of Service (DoS)

Denial of Service (DoS) attacks are one of the most feared forms of attack. Here the intruder wants to deny an organisation access to its own network or services. In doing so, that organisation is prevented from functioning – the longer it can be prevented from functioning, the less likely it is that the organisation will recover.

> **KEY CONCEPT**
>
> There are many threats to the network system – the majority coming from within the organisation. You need to be aware of these threats and be vigilant.

Elements of good practice

It is important that network security is viewed as a continuous process – new threats emerge daily and you must test to determine the effectiveness of your security. It should be based around a security policy. *Figure 12.1* shows the four essential steps in network security.

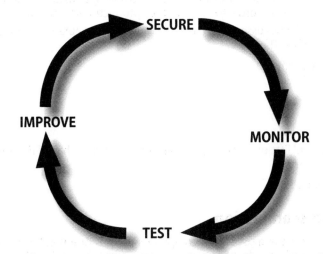

Figure 12.1: Major processes in network security (the security wheel)

In the first instance, an organisation needs to identify security objectives and resources to be protected. By using network maps, an effective security policy can be devised.

This policy can then be implemented (the secure part of *Figure 12.1*) using security devices such as firewalls, access control lists on a router, encryption and authentication devices (*see Section 2*).

Once the security policy has been implemented, the network needs to be monitored for access breaches or attacks. There are commercial pieces of software available to help you do this such as the Cisco Secure Intrusion Detection System. Such software will help you determine whether the network devices have been configured properly.

You will need to test the effectiveness of the safeguards you have put in place, against the security procedures that you devised. You may have developed the best security policy in the world but, unless you test it, you will never know whether it is working. Again software is available to help you do this e.g. Cisco's Security Scanner.

Finally, you will need to continually improve the security. You can only do this by collecting and analysing information, that has been gathered from the monitoring and testing phases. Don't forget, new vulnerabilities appear everyday.

You should regard security as a continuous process with all four steps being repeated continually and, where necessary, triggering amendments to the security policy.

> **KEY CONCEPT**
>
> Computer security is a continuous process of secure-monitor-test-improve and cannot be viewed as a single operation.

Section 2: Security technologies

The secure part of the security wheel requires the use of various technologies to help secure the organisation. No one technology will secure the organisation and it is important that you understand the technologies available so that you can best decide how to deploy them as part of the overall security strategy.

Introduction

Computer security is a major topic in computing and many millions of pounds are being spent by organisations in an attempt to keep their systems secure and by security technology developers in order to improve their products and secure their customers.

This chapter briefly discusses the major technologies available to help make organisations more secure. These are:

- physical disconnection;
- user accounts;
- NAT/PAT;
- firewalls;
- access control lists on a router (internal, upper and lower half of IP address range) DHCP from AAA;
- AAA security.

Physical disconnection

It is often said that the most secure computer system is one that has no network, is switched off and which is locked away securely, perhaps in a safe. Whilst this is true, such a computer system isn't particularly useful to an organisation. What is needed is an acceptable balance between this extreme security and the need for the organisation to access and use its data.

Such extreme security does provide a useful starting point for in evaluating what access to what data with which machine is actually needed. Useful questions can be asked such as:

- Does this machine need to be connected to the network? (Perhaps a PC running software such as PC anywhere server shouldn't be connected to the corporate network – as it is a potential security risk.)
- Does this machine need access to the whole network, for example should a student's PC in a college have access to the finance server?
- Do all employees need access to all data or can it be limited?
- Do we need to host our web pages? If they are only static, then you can reduce your risk by having them held on a third party server.

● Does everyone need access to the Internet or can they be given access to a restricted set of websites/web pages?

By answering these and similar questions you are able to determine more about the security requirements of the organisation (*see also Chapter 10, Risk assessment*).

User accounts

User accounts are sometimes overlooked as a security technology, but they form an essential part of your overall security policy. If two users share an account and fraud is detected from that account, how do you know who committed the fraud?

User accounts depend on education. You need to make sure that everyone understands the need to have and use their own account and to keep the user ID and password secure.

Accounts also provide the ability to tailor access to information. For example, a clerical assistant in a hospital may be allowed to see names and addresses of patients, but should they be allowed to see detailed medical records for that patient? Only by having everyone use their own accounts can the level of access be controlled.

Access control lists on a router

Access Control Lists (ACLs) on a router are a means by which traffic can be controlled based upon IP addresses. Traffic can be filtered on source address, destination address and port, giving network managers the ability to prevent unauthorised traffic from reaching a network. *Figure 12.2* shows a college whose student machines have the IP address range 192.168.1.x and whose finance machines have the IP address range 192.168.2.x. Normally traffic from the 192.168.1.x network will be allowed to flow through the router and to reach the 192.168.2.x network which contains the finance server. Placing an access control list on router A preventing access to the 192.18.2.x network from the 192.168.1.x will prevent the students from ever being able to reach the finance network. Better still would be to prevent all other networks from accessing the 192.168.2.x LAN.

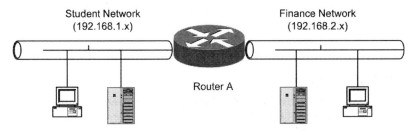

Student Network
(192.168.1.x)

Finance Network
(192.168.2.x)

Router A

Figure 12.2: A sample college LAN

An access control list (ACL) is usually placed on an interface. It is preferable to place ACLs as close to the source as possible to prevent traffic traversing the backbone only to be dropped when it reaches the destination. It is important to realise that an ACL drops the packet; there is simply no reply which gives an element of stealth to the protected network.

VLANs

Whilst the ACL example above prevents unauthorised access to the finance network, it relies on all of the finance department being located in one physical space with only one network serving it. Most modern organisations don't work on this model and instead have functions such as finance distributed across the entire organisation. For example, at the University of Sunderland, finance staff work in each school and most buildings.

The above example wouldn't support this operation. Instead, a VLAN model is required (see Chapter 1), which supports Virtual Local Area Networks across an organisation. Figure 12.3 shows the same college whose personnel, finance and student groups are spread across many buildings but using VLANs to keep the networks private. The router provides the ability for the VLANs to communicate with each other, but should have ACLs configured to prevent unauthorised access.

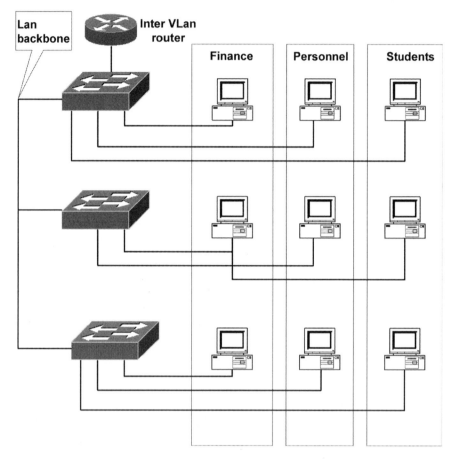

Figure 12.3: Using VLANs and Inter VLAN routing to secure functional areas distributed across an organisation

Network Address Translation (NAT)/Port Address Translation (PAT)

NAT and PAT are key elements in network security and are used to separate internal and external addressing schemes making it very difficult for a hacker on the outside to gain access to a computer on the inside. Figure 12.4 shows a typical deployment of NAT. The router sits between the organisation's internal network and the ISP. Computers on the inside of the network are using a private IP address range (as defined by RFC 1918). When a computer on the inside network wishes to communicate over the Internet, the router translates the internal private network IP address (192.168.1.1) to the external IP network address (157.228.1.1) – hence the term 'network address translation'. The packet originating from 192.168.1.1 cannot be routed over the Internet (as it is a private IP address) and has its source address replaced by that of the router before being placed on the Internet. The router keeps a table of internal and external mappings to use when a reply is received (Figure 12.5).

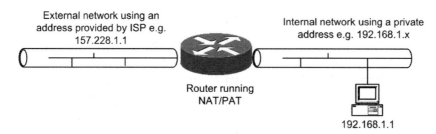

External network using an
address provided by ISP e.g.
157.228.1.1

Internal network using a private
address e.g. 192.168.1.x

Router running
NAT/PAT

192.168.1.1

Figure 12.4: A router using NAT/PAT connecting an internal and external network

Inside IP address	Outside IP address
192.168.1.1	157.228.1.1

Figure 12.5: Sample IP address mapping

When the reply is received, the router looks up the destination IP address in the map and translates it to the internal IP address before placing the packet on the internal network where it will be received by the machine that sent it. The translation can then be deleted from the map.

In this simple example, only one IP address is used for translation. This gives the restriction that only one internal computer can use the Internet at any one point in time – requests will be queued. In reality this solution wouldn't work and so a pool of external IP addresses can be defined that will allow a number of computers to access the Internet up to the maximum number of addresses in the pool.

In the case of smaller organisations or even in the home, only one IP address may be allocated preventing multiple computers from accessing the Internet at the same time. Another technique – Port Address Translation (PAT) is used to overcome this issue. PAT works in an identical fashion to NAT except that in addition to the IP address a port address is appended to the IP address. Port addresses are a normal part of an IP address, for example when we make a web request the port number 80 is automatically appended to the destination IP address. With PAT we are using unused source port numbers and appending them to the outside IP address. The router then maps the IP address and the port numbers and by using different port numbers for the different computers, it is able to allow multiple computers to share one IP address. *Figure 12.6* shows an example of this.

Inside IP address	Outside IP address
192.168.1.1	157.228.1.1:1024
192.168.1.2	157.228.1.1:1025

Figure 12.6: An example of PAT. Note two PCs now using the single IP address

The above examples show NAT being used dynamically for outbound traffic only. However, there are instances where we want NAT to be applied to inbound traffic. *Figure 12.7* shows a typical organisation with a web server. The web server needs to be accessible via a real IP address. In this case, one of the two IP addresses provided by the ISP is statically mapped using static NAT to the address of the web server (e.g. 157.228.1.2), the remaining one being used for dynamic NAT. Thus, 157.228.1.2 is statically mapped to 192.168.2.1. Any inbound packets to 157.228.1.2 will be translated to 192.168.2.1. 157.228.1.1 will be used for dynamic NAT outbound.

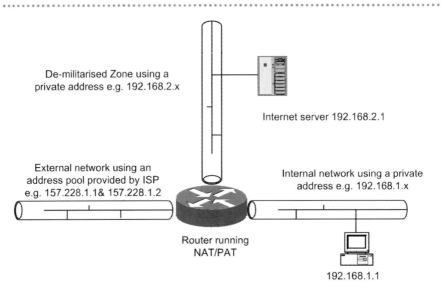

De-militarised Zone using a
private address e.g. 192.168.2.x

Internet server 192.168.2.1

External network using an
address pool provided by ISP
e.g. 157.228.1.1& 157.228.1.2

Internal network using a private
address e.g. 192.168.1.x

Router running
NAT/PAT

192.168.1.1

Figure 12.7: Typical deployment using static and dynamic NAT

Static NAT provides a means by which the web server can be accessed from a real IP address whilst the internal LAN is still protected. Notice that the Internet server is on a less secure network than the internal network – the so called De-Militarised Zone (DMZ).

KEY CONCEPT

NAT and PAT provide a means to hide your internal IP addresses and network and are usually the cornerstone of every security policy.

Firewall

There are generally three types of firewall available:

● hardware;

● software;

● specialist security appliance.

They are generally placed at network entrance to an organisation and are often either built into the border router itself (the so-called 'hardened router') or are a specialist security appliance (e.g. Cisco PIX range), which connects the internal and the external networks or are software on a computer. The function of a firewall is to examine packets (both sourced from internal and external addresses) and to apply pre-configured security policies to them. Usually the main function is to prevent hackers and harmful data from entering the organisation, although they can be configured to examine packet contents and prevent sensitive data leaving an organisation or prevent access to websites/traffic that don't meet the organisation's policy.

Of the three categories, software firewalls are generally considered to be the weakest. This is because they run upon an operating system that itself could be compromised. Thus if you had the best software firewall in the world, it could be defeated by attacking the operating system it runs on top of.

Hardware firewalls are much harder to defeat and are usually a router with an enhanced version of the router operating system. Whilst such devices are many more times harder to defeat than a software-based operating system, they are not as tough as a specialist security appliance.

Specialist security appliances, such as the Cisco PIX range, are designed from the outset for security with a secure operating system. Unlike a router that will allow traffic to flow unless configured not to, such devices deny traffic unless configured to allow it, making them the most secure type of firewall available. *Figure 12.8* shows a properly-secured organisational LAN.

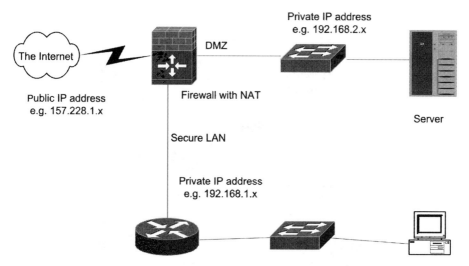

Figure 12.8: A properly-secured organisational LAN

AAA authentication/syslog servers

Obviously, security can be compromised if intruders manage to obtain access to key networking devices. First and foremost, key networking devices should be physically secure – most can have their passwords reset if you have physical access to them!

AAA (Authentication, Authorisation and Accounting) servers provide security to key networking devices. Using AAA servers, anyone wanting to log into a key networking device must be authenticated by a secure server.

The authorisation part of AAA is relatively straight forward – is the user allowed access to this device? Then authorisation determines the level of access the user has to that device, for example are they allowed to view or change the configuration. Finally the accounting part writes a secure audit trail of every entry and change that has been made. Often the audit trail has to be written before the change can be made.

There are three types of secure server:

1. Kerberos;

2. RADIUS;

3. TACACS+.

RADIUS and TACACS+ are the two predominant AAA servers. TACACS+ is Cisco proprietary where RADIUS is open standard. RADIUS is currently the only one supporting wireless LANs.

Syslog servers hold another form of audit trail – normally a key networking device displays a message of every change made on the computer being used to make the change. This information can form a crucial audit trail and so can be copied to a syslog server to give a more permanent record. A syslog server is nothing more than a piece of software running on a PC.

Network time servers

In a secure network it is important that the clocks on all network devices are kept in sync. Any audit trails written to logging devices are much more useful if the time stamp is accurate providing a means by which the network manager can correlate the audit trail to specific events. Network Time Servers (NTSs) use the Network Time Protocol (NTP) and are used to synchronise the times on all network devices; the synchronisation usually comes from a satellite using an atomic clock (*Figure 12.9*).

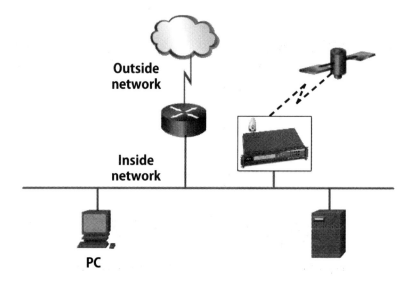

Figure 12.9: Typical NTS usage (image courtesy of Cisco Systems Inc.)

> **KEY CONCEPT**
>
> Networking is critical to most organisations and security is crucial to networking. Treat security seriously!

Section 3: End of chapter assessment

Questions

These questions relate to the assessment targets set at the beginning of this chapter. If you can answer them effectively you are in a good position to achieve good credit in assessments or examinations.

1. Outline the need for network security and discuss elements of good practice.

2. Name the major security technologies and for each briefly discuss its operation and detail how it increases security.

Answers

1. As you are aware, computer security is of paramount importance and is cause for concern for most organisations. In answering this question, you need to highlight the critical importance of computer security, which may be helped by making comparisons to a paper-based method.

   You should briefly mention the possible threats to a computer-based system before going on to outline the elements of good practice. I would recommend that you draw the 'security wheel' outlined in *Figure 12.1* and discuss each of the steps. It is important that you highlight that computer security is a continuous process and must be treated as such – don't forget that new threats appear almost daily.

2. For each technology you should discuss how the technology operates and how it provides network security. To gain extra marks, highlight any advantages/ disadvantages to using the technology and give examples of where the technology could be used and where it should be placed in the network for maximum effect.

    You can also impress the assessor by highlighting that the security technologies should be used as part of a co-ordinated security strategy and that by using them piecemeal it is likely to compromise their effect.

Section 4: Further reading and research

Cisco Networking Academy Program (2003), CCNA 3 and 4 *Companion Guide*, (3rd edn). Cisco Press. ISBN: 1 58713 113 7. Chapters 11 and 16.

www.freeradius.org

www.gnu.org/software/radius/radius.html

Glossary

ACL Access Control List.

ADSL Asymmetric Digital Subscriber Line.

AP Access Point (wireless).

ARP Address Resolution Protocol.

ASCII American Standard Code for Information Interchange.

backbone (cabling) – this is the cabling that connects the main network components – for example, switches, routers, etc. It forms the backbone of the network. Sometimes called vertical cabling.

baud – the measure of the number of times a signal varies per second. Often confused with bits per second as early systems encoded one bit per signal variation. Modern systems encode multiple bits on a signal variation.

bit Binary digIT, a 1 or a 0 – the basic level at which computers operate.

bps Bits per second – a measure of throughput usually related to networks. The number of bits per second that can be/are transferred.

Broadcast storm – this is an excessive transmission of broadcast packets in a network which can cause serious network performance issues.

BSA Basic Service Area (Wireless LANs).

Cat 3 – telephone cable that cannot handle high-speed data. Techniques can be used to improve performance, such as ADSL.

Cat 5 – this is the most common form of cabling in networking. Most new buildings are wired using this cable. It is capable of handling data transmission at 100 Mbps.

CRC Cyclic Redundancy Check – an error-detection mechanism.

DNS Domain Name Server – this is the network server that converts the URL into an IP number.

DMZ De-Militarised Zone.

EISA Extended Industry Standard Architecture – a popular architecture used in computers since the 1990s.

flow control – the ability to restrict the flow of information to accommodate slower devices on the network.

FTP File Transfer Protocol – used to send files across a computer network.

Gbps Gigabits per second (1000 Mbps).

GE Gigabit Ethernet.

Horizontal cabling – cabling from IDF/MDF to desktop.

HTTP HyperText Transfer Protocol – used to transfer web pages across a network.

IDF Intermediate Distribution Facility – a point on the floor where network equipment and wiring is located.

IP Internet Protocol – the networking protocol that is used on the Internet.

IP number – in version 4, a 4-byte dotted decimal number (e.g. 157.228.102.1) which represents the logical address of a computer on the Internet.

ISA Industry Standard Architecture – the first internal PC architecture used by IBM-compatible PCs.

Mb Megabits.

MB Megabytes – different from megabits.

Mbps Megabits per second – different from megabytes. Also written as Mbit/s.

MLS or **MPLS** Multiprotocol Layer Switch

MCA Micro Channel Architecture – an internal PC architecture developed by IBM for its PS/2 and RS6000 range of computers.

MDF Main Distribution Facility – the first distribution facility in a building where networking equipment is located and wiring terminates. Usually houses POP.

NAT Network Address Translation.

NIC Network Interface Card.

NOS Networked Operating System (e.g. Novell).

Parity An error-detection mechanism – a bit is added to the end of a series of bits (usually a byte) to permit an error in the transmission to be detected.

PAT Port Address Translation.

PCI Peripheral Component Interconnect – an Intel-devised internal computer architecture that provides much greater speeds than either ISA or EISA.

PCMCIA – the architecture used by laptops and other small devices – credit card-sized interface cards.

POP Point-of-Presence – the actual location houses telecommunication and networking equipment.

RSM Router Switch Module.

Server farm – centralised location of all an organisations servers.

SMTP Simple Mail Transfer Protocol – used by mail servers to exchange email.

STP Shielded twisted pair cabling – more immune to interference than UTP.

TCP Transmission Control Protocol – the transmission control method used by the Internet.

10GE 10 Gigabit Ethernet.

TFTP Trivial File Transfer Protocol – used for small files. Less reliable than FTP.

URL Uniform Resource Locator – a web address (e.g. cisco.sunderland.ac.uk).

USB Universal Serial Bus – a high-speed serial interface.

USB2 – a faster version of USB.

UTP Unshielded Twisted Pair cabling – widely used in modern installations.

Vertical cabling *see backbone (cabling)*

VLAN Virtual LAN – a protocol enabling a LAN to be divided into several virtual LANs.

VoIP Voice Over Internet Protocol

VPN Virtual Private Network – a protocol for establishing (virtual) private networks over the Internet.

WAP Wireless Access Point.

WiFi – same as WLAN.

Wiring closet – *see IDF*

Wireless bridge – using a wireless LAN to bridge two other LANs.

WLAN Wireless Local Area Network – a wire-free networking solution.

Index